Thomas Rennell

A Sermon Preached in the Cathedral Church of St. Paul, London

On Thursday, June 6, 1799

Thomas Rennell

A Sermon Preached in the Cathedral Church of St. Paul, London
On Thursday, June 6, 1799

ISBN/EAN: 9783744745390

Printed in Europe, USA, Canada, Australia, Japan

Cover: Foto ©Lupo / pixelio.de

More available books at **www.hansebooks.com**

A

S E R M O N

Preached in the CATHEDRAL CHURCH of

ST. PAUL, LONDON:

On THURSDAY, JUNE 6, 1799.

BEING THE TIME

Of the YEARLY MEETING of the
CHILDREN Educated in the CHARITY-
SCHOOLS, in and about the Cities of LONDON
and WESTMINSTER.

BY

THOMAS RENNELL, D.D. F.A.S.

MASTER OF THE TEMPLE.

Publifhed at the Requeſt of the SOCIETY FOR PROMOTING
CHRISTIAN KNOWLEDGE,
And the TRUSTEES of the feveral SCHOOLS.

To which is annexed,

AN ACCOUNT OF THE
SOCIETY FOR PROMOTING CHRISTIAN KNOWLEDGE.

LONDON:

Printed by ANN RIVINGTON, PRINTER TO THE SAID
SOCIETY, in ST. JOHN'S-SQUARE, CLERKENWELL.

FRANCIS and CHARLES RIVINGTON, at (N° 62,)
the BIBLE and CROWN, in ST. PAUL's CHURCH-YARD, &c.
the SOCIETY's Bookfellers.

M DCC XCIX.

[iii]

CONTENTS.

" Whoever wishes to become a Member of *the Society for promoting Christian Knowledge*, or to make any enquiry concerning it, is requested to write to the *Rev. Dr.* G A S K I N, *Secretary to the Society, Bartlett's Buildings, Holborn, London*, who will give him every necessary information and direction."

GALATIANS vi. 7.

WHATSOEVER A MAN SOWETH THAT SHALL HE
ALSO REAP.

THE connection between caufes and effects
in various branches of natural, political, and
moral philofophy, in the cultivation of fcience and
the improvement of art, occupies much of our
thought and attention. In fome, and thofe not a
few inftances, our inveftigation becomes, in the
prefent frame of the minds of men, either fo refined by metaphyfical abftraction, or fo mifapplied
by feeble and impertinent curiofity, as to pafs into
a fpecies of abufe. We fatigue our faculties in
endeavouring to penetrate into fubjects where the
great Author of Nature has interpofed infurmount-
able barriers to human petulance and prefumption.
But while we ftrain our fight, in vain *efforts* to ex-

a   plore

plore objects diftant and indiftinct, we neglect to
read thofe characters which God has engraved upon
our hearts and confciences ; we overlook what common fenfe has fuggefted, experience confolidated,
and fcripture, which is invariably in perfect unifon
with both, hath fealed and fanctioned.

There is no connection between moral actions
and their confequences, more diftinct and palpable,
nor any one more neglected both in theory and practice, than that which refults from the communi-
cation of religious knowledge among the young, the
ignorant, and the uncultivated. Politicians, not
warned either by a confideration of the ftructure of
man, the tenor of hiftorical fact, or the laws upon
which the whole moral fyftem of Providence pro-
ceeds, I fear are ftill *wilfully ignorant*, that, whatever
may be the refources of a nation, in riches, popula-
tion, and commerce, however wifely its form of government may be adjufted, however it may be de-
fended by the valour of its hofts and the wifdom of
its councils, yet if its moral and religious foundation
is not deep and firm, its exiftence lies at the mercy

of

of the *flighteft* accident ; however fortified againſt *external* violence, yet from *internal* tumults it can never be fecure. Nothing but the fear of God, and the ſtability of morals which this fear imparts, can ſo calm the affections and regulate the paſſions of men, as to give permanency to national exiſtence and fe-curity. We need not therefore hefitate to affert, in diſtinct oppoſition to one of the favourite maxims of that Political Philofophy, which has in theſe days threatened the ruin of the whole human race, that the chriſtian legiſlator is ſtrictly bound to promote, to protect, and incorporate with his civil polity, the genuine religion of Jeſus Chriſt. For ſo far it is from being true that civil polity is a ſubject *unconnected* with religion, that on the contrary, reli-gion is its *eſſence*, and the *very baſis* upon which it reſts. And not only is the magiſtrate bound to give chriſtianity *general* protection and eſtabliſhment, but he is bound likewiſe to watch all the *particular* channels by which it may be diffuſed and diſſemi-nated. And upon the fame principle, all thofe who wiſh well to their country, are called upon to the promotion of every undertaking which has this

a 2   ſalutary

falutary and important objeÉt for its end. In a *ge-*
neral view, there is no one whom the effeÉts of national profligacy may not reach : no one fo high, fo
fecure, but muft in his *private* conneÉtions, as well
as in his *public* capacity, be warned by all the ftu-
pendous movements of divine Providence, which
have fhaken the whole foundations of the moral
world in every quarter of the globe, that " *God is
not mocked,*" and that " *whatever a man foweth that
fhall he alfo reap.*"

Under a conviÉtion that in thefe few general and
obvious refleÉtions, I am anticipated by thofe, who
are engaged in the defign of this day's folemnity ;
I fhall concifely direÉt your attention in the following
difcourfe,   Firft,

To the circumftances of the times, in which the
ignorance of Chriftianity is to be remedied and prevented.   Secondly,

To the fpecific exertions, by which this has been
attempted by the members of this inftitution ; and
Thirdly,

                                        To

To the duty of zealously co-operating with this work of charity, and labour of love.

Although in *all* times there appears a sufficient degree of that apostacy from God, which the primæval defection from him engendered in our fallen nature, yet this corruption does in a marvellous degree assimilate itself to the various political opinions, and social habits, of *particular* ages of the world. The evil consequences arising from these, it is the peculiar object of religious instruction to remedy and counteract. Upon political opinions and principles, I will only observe, that errors more fatal, and mistakes more radical, have prevailed in the times in which we live, than in any former period of the annals of the human race. As *civil governors* throughout Europe, did not condescend to make Religion the stability of their power; so the *governed* on their part, seeing how lightly religion was prized, by those invested with authority, gave into a profligate opinion, that civil government was the *creature* of the *people*, and not the INSTITUTION of GOD. This under different shapes received

great

great encouragement from thofe, who expected a rich harveft from the confufions and diftractions, which the general acceptance of fuch opinions promifed to produce. The prevalence of thefe fentiments reduced the wretched countries where they were firft broached, to a wreck and ruin ; and had nearly, if Providence had not vifibly interpofed, precipitated the reft of Europe into the gulph of the fame deftruction.

There is no occafion to dwell upon events before us all. It is fufficient to fay, that what *fuperftition* was incapable of doing in France and Italy, the Chriftianity of this PROTESTANT nation has here effected. To the principles therefore diffufed by the labours of this Society, we are, under God, principally to look for the prefervation of the country. But this will moft powerfully be effected, by a diffemination of true and fcriptural doctrines, upon the obedience due, from *chriftian fubjects*, to *chriftian magiftrates*. All we have feen, all we have feared, all we have felt for thefe laft ten years, leads us to promote the furtherance of that religion, which enjoins its true difciples " *whatever city they enter into, to pray for*
the

the peace of that city;" to *" render unto all their dues, fear to whom fear, honour to whom honour, tribute to whom tribute."*

Another circumftance of the times which renders the labours of this Society of peculiar exigency, is the moft lamentable and notorious defectivenefs of chriftian education in many of our public fchools, and other great feminaries of this nation [A]. In thofe happy times, when men in the higher and middle ranks *neceffarily* imbibed in the courfe of their education the effential principles of the Gofpel, while thefe were made an *integral* part of the fyftems of general inftruction, every mafter of a family in his turn became a teacher to his domeftics, to his children, and to his neighbours. What he *freely* received he *freely* imparted. But all who are acquainted with the elementary ignorance of chriftianity, in which young men are permitted to remain, in the greater part of our public inftitutions, (and it is impoffible to be much converfant in them without knowing this) will fee how neceffary the exertions of *this* Society are for preferving the light of the

Gofpel,

Gofpel, among the lower ranks of men. Ignorance and irreligion are extremely apt to defcend from the high to the low; and therefore when the refervoirs which ufed to diffufe thefe falutary ftreams among thofe of elevated rank are choaked and dried up, the charitable hand which fupplies the deficiency among the poor, is peculiarly grateful to God and beneficial to mankind.

Still greater if poffible, and more ftrenuous exertion is called for, from the progrefs of riotous and diffipated revelry, which has for years been incalculably encreafing among us, and appears in the prefent moment to amount to an intoxicated defiance of every principle of public welfare and private virtue. Concerning the influence of thefe profligate nocturnal meetings upon the morals of thofe who *exhibit* and furnifh them, it is not my prefent purpofe to defcant; or to enquire how grateful a return this is to that gracious Providence, which has fo vifibly interfered in ftaying the hands of the avenging angel! But to confider their effects direct and indirect upon the morals of the lower ranks of men, is

4   indeed

indeed a very awful fubject of reflection. To what
are the numerous domeftics of thefe men configned
over, during fuch feftivities, but to the oaths, and
drunkennefs, the debauchery, riot and confufion,
which the ftreets of a populous and luxurious Me-
tropolis exhibit! While this proftration of religious
principle, is every day by the high and affluent
effected among their domeftics and dependants, how
bleffed are thofe labours, which may in fome meafure
counteract fuch baleful confequences! The principles taught in *thefe* Schools, the plain and powerful
admonitions contained in the tracts fo widely difperfed by our Society, may by God's providence arreft
many, who otherwife might have perifhed in that
gulph, to the brink of which, thofe who *ought* to
have been their guides to happinefs and falvation,
have profligately and unfeelingly conducted them.

Having thus pointed to the peculiar *obftacles*,
which the Patrons of this charitable Inftitution
have to contend with; I have briefly, in order to
recommend them to general protection and pa-
b   tronage,

tronage, to advert to the manner in which their defigns are anfwered.

The firft, is the *early* inftruction in religious truth, communicated by them. A certain foolifh and foppifh opinion, derived from, and intimately connected with modern philofophy, has lately gone forth, that religion is the bufinefs of *maturer* years only, and that early culture is productive not of rational conviction, but of blind prejudice. I can fcarcely be of opinion, that we fhould admire or imitate the wifdom of the hufbandman, who fhould *fow* his *feed* at the feafon, when it is time to *reap* the *fruits.* To the refined folly of the propagators of this maxim, we may confidently oppofe the plain and practical words of fcripture, " *Train up a child in the way that he fhould go, and when he is old he will not depart from it.*"

Another means by which the benevolent ends of this charity is anfwered, is by habituating thefe children, to an early and lafting fenfe of the SANCTITY OF THE SABBATH. I have no hefitation in afferting

most

moſt unequivocally, that upon the ſerious, ſubſtan-
tial, and effective obſervation of this ſacred day, the
whole edifice of Religion reſts as its ſtrongeſt pillar.
In the ſupport of this *primary* ordinance, of *all* religion, PATRIARCHAL, MOSAIC, and CHRISTIAN, too
great a portion of our zeal, courage, and activity,
cannot poſſibly be expended. *Here* a vigorous ſtand
is to be made, againſt the enemies of chriſtianity :
and it is with great ſatisfaction we obſerve,
that God, who in the worſt of times, never leaves
himſelf without witneſſes, has raiſed up ſome even
in the higheſt ranks, who have deciſively, boldly,
and manfully, in ſteady oppoſition to refined pert-
neſs, profligate ridicule, hardened buffoonery, and
profane virulence, directed the attention of the legi-
ſlature to this important object [B].

Another powerful means of preſerving and dif-
fuſing true religion among the maſs of the people,
is by preſerving with unremitting anxiety, the doctrines of our truly PRIMITIVE AND APOSTOLICAL
ENGLISH CHURCH. Notwithſtanding the love of
many, in theſe days of apoſtacy, hath waxed cold,

not

notwithſtanding thé rapid progreſs which luxury,, indolence, and diſſipation, has made among all orders, and profeſſions of men, notwithſtanding the inceſſant artifices of infidelity, difguifed under the maſk of *liberality, candour*, and *free enquiry*, God hath ſtill preſerved to us without decay, ad-mixture, or depravation, that FULL body of chriſtian verity, which our primitive reformers framed by their wifdom, and fealed with their blood. And we ſhould do well to remember, that *doctrine* is the very vital fubſtance of the church, that which every other part of the ecclefiaftical fabric is defigned to protect and preſerve. Without this a church is a dead and putrid carcafs, cumbering the ground in which it is planted, its ceremonies are idle mockery, and its miniſters burthenfome and ufelefs ſtipendiaries to the public. The preſervation of the purity of our faith therefore, and the diffufion of it in its genuine integrity, is of the higheſt confequence to the intereſts of real chriſtianity in this nation. In proportion to the excellency of the faith maintained in the Engliſh church, its warfare with the powers of darkneſs on every fide, has been

continued

continued and vigorous; and its conteft remains even to this day. It is befet by the fcoffs of infidels, and the knavery of enthufiafts; it has to combat with the arts, virulence, and inceffant activity of POPERY, which in a fifter kingdom had lately nearly effected the deftruction of the Proteftant eftablifhment, and which the agents of that antichriftian fuperftition, are now exerting in every quarter of *this kingdom*, with a greater cunning, and more extended fuccefs, than at any period fince the reformation [c]. But we truft that through the channel of this Society, the principles of our church againft *all* its foes have been and will be afferted, and its doctrines fcrupuloufly guarded. The piety and morality taught by it, is of a firm, manly, durable, and truly evangelical texture; promoting *chriftian practice* upon *chriftian principles*, and honeftly and *unequivocally* adding to faith, virtue, and to zeal, knowledge, and to fervor, fobriety. The check given to the whims, the enervation, the folly, and the petulance of enthufiafm has been very confiderable; this has been done, as it ever will be moft effectually, not by the lukewarmnefs of what is commonly called *rational divi-*

nity,

nity, but by the fervent piety and genuine ortho-
doxy, which breathes in the writings of our old
Englifh theologians.

By the labours and exertions of the SOCIETY FOR
THE PROMOTING CHRISTIAN KNOWLEDGE, the
departed minifters of Chrift " *though dead yet
fpeak.*". The voice of KETTLEWELL, of BEVERIDGE,
of KENN, and of TILLOTSON, yet calls us from
their tombs to practical holinefs, and to " *flee from
the wrath to come.*" By the ineftimable exertions
of this numerous Society, fo peculiarly bleffed by
the favour and protection of God, more perhaps
than by any other *fingle* means, the genuine light of
the Gofpel is preferved, and the wreck of the civil
and ecclefiaftical fabric, under Providence, prevented.
The character, the good-nature, the franknefs, the
integrity of Englifhmen, I have no fcruple to affert,
have hitherto *left* flourifhed in the bofom of the
eftablifhed Church ; and that *all* diffent from it, has
a ftrong tendency at leaft to *disfigure*, if not to
deftroy thefe genuine and characteriftic features of
the national virtues and difpofition.

I fhall

I fhall now very briefly urge the reward, attendant upon a co-operation with this day's labour of love, in prefervation of thefe poor innocents from the contagion of vice, and mifery, which is attendant upon a ftate of religious ignorance. And furely here, I have no occafion for any force of *words*, to bring home to your hearts and confciences, the rich reward, temporal and eternal, of co-operating with this work of faith. Before the prefent fpectacle, the hardeft heart muft melt, and the moft obdurate infidelity be converted, into the " *wifdom of the juft*." If in the fight of God every one of the fouls of thefe children is precious, if in Heaven their angels " *do always behold the face of their Father, which is in Heaven*," how urgent the duty, how rich the reward of delivering them from the tremendous confequences of fin and mifery! How painful and dreadful the thought, that of thefe little ones, any of the one fex, fhould be the victims of proftitution and all its namelefs horrors; and of the other, numbers fhould perifh under the ftroke of public juftice in this life, and fuffer the more awful vengeance of God in the next. Surely at the hands of

I　　　　　　　　　　　　　　　thofe,

thofe, who are corrupting them by their vices, who in
the midft of affluence, turn a deaf ear to the voice of
thefe poor children's fupplication, will God require
their blood! And furely, if there be a fpectacle, which
God can bow down from Heaven to behold, if
there be a fpectacle at all approaching to that
beatific vifion, which fhall be revealed to the fpirits
of the juft made perfect, it is that now before us !
So many innocent fouls preferved from fin and per-
dition, co-heirs with us of life and immortality !
This is indeed a victory over fin, death, and hell !
This, by fecuring a future harveft of piety and virtue in the rifing generation, can alone confolidate,
by the blefling of God, any *other* meafures which
human policy may dictate for the prefervation
of this Proteftant church and nation. Surely
the apocalyptic vifion burfts in upon us, in the
prefent moment, in all its awe, majefty, and fplen-
dor. " *I John, faw the holy city, the new Jerufalem,*
coming down from God out of Heaven, prepared as
a bride adorned for her hufband; and I heard a great
voice out of Heaven, faying, Behold the tabernacle of
God is with men, and he will dwell with them, and

they

they fhall be his people, and God himfelf fhall be with them and be their God!" May we, in conjunction with our own deareft relatives, be thought worthy, through the merits of the Mediator, to join thefe poor children, now arrayed in the *" white robes"* of innocency before us, in a haven of everlafting blifs and confolation, and to worfhip before the throne of God through all eternity, *" with the great multitude which no man can number, of all nations and kindreds, and people, and tongues ; faying, Salvation unto our God which fitteth upon the throne, and to the Lamb: —Bleffing, and glory, and wifdom, and thankfgiving, and honour, and power, and might, be unto our God for ever and ever."*

c NOTES.

NOTES.

[A] THE *general* state of public education in this country, with regard to religion, appears to require much attention. We cannot but lament, that in *very few* of our best endowed seminaries, the study of Christianity has that portion of time and regard allotted to it, which the welfare of society, the progress of delusive and ruinous errors, and the true interest of sound learning itself, seems at the present time, *peculiarly* to call for. In *some* of them, and those not of *small* celebrity or importance, *all* consideration of the revealed will of God is passed over with a resolute, systematic, and contemptuous neglect, which is not exceeded in that which the French call their *national institute*. And yet with every branch of learning, the study of the Holy Scriptures is closely connected : with history, chronology, criticism, and morals, none of which, if the Bible be excluded, can be carried to their full perfection. How far those whose occupation it is to form the national taste can be warranted, even in *this* point of view, in such conduct, may be collected from ONE, whose opinion on every subject relating to polite literature is decisive.—" The " collection of tracts which we call, from their excellence, the " Scriptures, contain, independently of a divine origin, more *true* " *sublimity*, more *exquisite beauty*, *purer morality*, more *important history*, " and *finer strains both of poetry and eloquence*, than could be collected " within the same compass from all *other books* that were ever " composed in any age, or in any idiom."—SIR WILLIAM JONES'S *Eighth Dissertation in the Asiatic Researches.*

The consequence of this neglect will be, as indeed is already evident, that *learning itself* deprived of the blessing of Almighty God, and having lost its main pillar, his fear and support, must rapidly decline. Indolence and dissipation, even in *these* retreats, will have their perfect work, and in a short period even the very *form* and *external* appearance of discipline and instruction will perish. *Industry* and *dignity* in those who *teach*, and *subordination* and *readily* in those who *learn*, cannot long survive the PRINCIPLE, which alone gives permanency to them all.

But

NOTES,

But in the prefent moral and political ſtate of human affairs, the conſequences are *immediately* alarming. Young men of rank and talents are diſmiſſed into the world, without *one ſingle* ſafe-guard againſt thoſe plauſible and tremendous theories, which have turned more than one quarter of the world into an Aceldama, or field of blood! Of religion, its evidences, doctrines, and motives, they are utterly and groſsly ignorant : No check therefore, reſtraint, or corrective is afforded from hence ; they are therefore, not unfrequently, hurried on by heated imaginations and enflamed pride, *aggravated* rather than *controuled* by the learning they have acquired, to turn the arms of eloquence and genius to the ſub-verſion of order, and the deſtruction of their native country. Young men in this ſituation are not unemphatically deſcribed by *Cicero :*—" Quâ cæcitate homines, cum quædam etiam præclara
" cuperent, eaque *neſcirent* nec ubi, nec qualia eſſent, *funditus*
" *alii everterunt ſuas civitates*, alii ipſi occiderunt. Atque hi qui-
" dem *optima* petentes, non tam *voluntate*, quam *curſus errore* fal-
" luntur."—*Cicero Tuſc. Quæſt.*

This evil however, for which PAGANISM ſupplied no remedy, CHRISTIANITY, by abating the preſumption, and ſoftening the af-fections of men, would, if inculcated at an *early* period of life, effectually counteract. CHRISTIANITY alone can peculiarly, in the preſent diſpoſition of the minds of men, turn learning and talents into a bleſſing to this country. There is ſcarcely an *interna* danger which we fear, but what is to be aſcribed to a *pagan* edu-cation, under *Chriſtian eſtabliſhments*, in a *Chriſtian* country. If thoſe who preſide over our public ſeminaries, ſhould be ever awakened to their deep reſponſibility in this important duty to GOD, their KING, and their COUNTRY ; *then*, in the awful words of the reverend and venerable Mr. *Jones*, in a late publication, entitled,
" Conſiderations on the Religious Worſhip of the Heathen :"—" we
" ſhall not be long under the dominion of profligate ſcholars, who uſe
" their heathen learning for no end, but as an inſtrument of evil,
" to corrupt and deſtroy the Chriſtian world ; increaſing all that
" miſery daily, which abounds too much already."

9   [B] This

NOTES.

[n] This alludes to a moſt laudable effort of the Right Hon. Lord Belgrave, to prevent a wanton and licentious profanation of the Sabbath, in vending and diſtributing Newſpapers on that day.

[c] For a view of the rapid and extended progreſs of popery in England, I refer the reader to his own obſervation, of the numerous, and daily increaſing popiſh ſeminaries, ſchools, monaſteries, nunneries, and the diſtribution of cheap elementary tracts, in every part of this iſland. This is exhibited in the fulleſt manner, by the Papiſts themſelves, in an annual publication, entitled, The Laity's Directory, printed for J. Coghlan, Duke-ſtreet, Groſvenor-ſquare, a popiſh bookſeller. This regiſter will point out, beyond poſſibility of doubt, the ſpread and ramifications of the miſchief we have to contend with. For the ſanguinary and dreadful effects of this ſuperſtition in Ireland, during the late rebellion, I refer my readers to Dr. Duigenan's recent publication, entitled, "A Fair Repreſentation of the preſent Political State of Ireland." I here repeat, what I have before had occaſion to aſſert *, that I know no man by whom the Proteſtant cauſe has been ſerved with equal manlineſs, ability, and effect. His views of popery correſpond with thoſe exhibited by TILLOTSON, SECKER, and SHERLOCK. He underſtands the principles of the Romiſh church as ſhe herſelf profeſſes them : he has exhibited them from documents, which no Papiſt will diſavow; he has ſhewn their practice from facts, which no Papiſt can controvert.

——— Quæque ipſe miſerrima vidit
Et quorum pars magna fuit !

Upon every principle on which our Society is founded, and by which it is cemented, the peruſal and recommendation of this moſt intereſting tract, is a matter of the higheſt importance and obligation.

* Vide a Sermon entitled, "Ignorance productive of Atheiſm, Anarchy, and Superſtition," preached before the Univerſity of Cambridge, on Commencement Sunday, 1799, and printed by Deſire of the Heads of Houſes;—By the Author of this Diſcourſe.

AN

ACCOUNT

OF THE

SOCIETY

FOR PROMOTING

CHRISTIAN KNOWLEDGE.

LONDON:

Printed by ANNE RIVINGTON, PRINTER TO THE SAID
SOCIETY, in ST. JOHN's-SQUARE, CLERKENWELL;

And fold by FRANCIS and CHARLES RIVINGTON,
BOOKSELLERS, at the BIBLE and CROWN, N° 62,
ST. PAUL's CHURCH-YARD.

1799.

A N

A C C O U N T

OF THE

SOCIETY FOR PROMOTING CHRISTIAN KNOWLEDGE.

THE SOCIETY FOR PROMOTING CHRIS-TIAN KNOWLEDGE, were, for many Years, engaged in carrying on fuch Defigns, as they judged might promote the Interefts of true Religion, and the Honour of Almighty GOD, by whofe Blefling this good Work has been continually prof-pering in their Hands; but, finding that their De-figns were not fo generally known as they could wifh, and confequently not fo much encouraged as it was prefumed they would be, when further known, they refolved not only to publifh an Ac-count of them, but alfo to communicate to the World, from Year to Year, their Proceedings, and the State of their Affairs.

A 2   This

THIS SOCIETY confifts chiefly of SUB-SCRIBING, and partly of CORRE-SPONDING Members; who, before they can be chofen, muft be recommended in the *Form* N° I. in the *Appendix*. Of the former, you have a complete Lift, under the fame Number, in the *Appendix*. They fubfcribe fuch annual Sums as every one thinks proper, towards fupporting the Expences of the Society; and have their regular Meetings, 'in which all Bufinefs, relating thereunto, is tranfacted. And as moft of thefe, when this Society was firft formed, lived in or near *London*, they were then, and until *A. D.* 1727, called RESIDING Members. The latter are fuch Perfons, in *Great-Britain* and *Ireland*, and other Proteftant Countries, as are chofen to correfpond with the Society, on Purpofe to acquaint them with the State of Religion in their Neighbourhood; to fuggeft fuch Methods of doing Good as occur to them; to diftribute Bibles, with fuch religious, as well as ufeful Books, as fhall be approved of, and recommended by the Society; and to remit any occafional Benefactions, which they are pleafed to contribute themfelves, or collect from well difpofed Chriftians.

But for the better underftanding the Nature and Defigns of this Society, it is thought convenient to premife a fhort Narrative of its Rife and Progrefs. ——It was about the latter End of the Year 1698, when a few Gentlemen formed themfelves into a *Voluntary Society:* And as fuch, they with Unanimity and Zeal went on together in promoting the real and practical Knowledge of true Religion, by fuch Methods as appeared to them, from Time to Time, to be moft conducive to that End, till towards the Conclufion

1698.
The Original of the Society.

clufion of the Year 1701 ; when, at their Inftance, 1701.
a CHARTER was obtained from King WILLIAM III.
whereby all the then Subfcribing Members of this
Society, with other Perfons of Diftinction in Church
and State, were Incorporated, for the better carrying *Of the Incor-*
on that Branch of their Defigns, which related to *poratedSociety*
for Propaga-
the *Plantations, Colonies,* and *Factories beyond the tionoftheGof-*
Seas, belonging to the Kingdom of England. *pel in Foreign*
Parts.

BUT their CHARTER being limited to *Foreign* TheIncorpo-
Parts, and the Bufinefs of that Corporation being rated Society
being limited
hitherto confined to the *Britifh* Plantations in *America,* to the *Britifh*
moft of the Original Members of our *Voluntary So- Plantations,*
ciety ftill continued to carry on, in that Capacity, the Original
Members
their more extenfive Defigns for advancing the Ho- continue as a
nour of GOD, and the Good of Mankind, by pro- *Voluntary So-*
ciety.
moting Chriftian Knowledge, both at Home and in
other Parts of the World, by the beft Methods that
fhould offer. They are therefore a Society diftinct
from that *Corporation,* and are known by the Name
of THE SOCIETY FOR PROMOTING CHRISTIAN
KNOWLEDGE.

THEIR principal Methods were the fame as they
had been before. The FIRST was to procure and
encourage the erecting of CHARITY-SCHOOLS, in all Charity-
Parts of the Kingdom : and, that thofe Schools might Schools
erected.
anfwer the true Purpofes, for which they were erected, the Society have not been wanting (in their Cor-
refpondence with fuch of their Members as have been
concerned in the Support and Management thereof)
to recommend, at all Times, that, together with Religious and ufeful Inftruction, Care fhould be taken,
and all proper Means ufed, to inure the Children of
the Poor to Induftry and Labour, that fo they may
become good Chriftians, loyal and ufeful Subjects,

8   and

and be willing, as well as fit, to be employed not only in Trades or Services, but alfo in Hufbandry, Navigation, or any other Bufinefs, that fhall be thought of moft Ufe, and Benefit, to the Public. With thefe Views, the Society printed, and difperfed, fuch a Set of Rules, for the good Order and Governmentof thefe Schools, as had been approved of by the Archbifhops and Bifhops, who directed that the fame fhould be obferved, within their refpective Diocefes. What Care they have taken, and what they have done, in thefe Particulars, will appear from N° II. in the *Appendix*.

Bibles, Prayer-Books, &c. difperfed. ANOTHER Method was to difperfe, both at Home and Abroad, Bibles, Prayer-Books, and divers Sorts of Religious Tracts : and accordingly they have, by the Affiftance of their Members, difperfed an incredible Number of them, in fuch a Manner as, they have Reafon to hope, has tended to the great Increafe of the Knowledge and Practice of our holy Religion. Thefe Books and Tracts (of which there is a Catalogue in the *Appendix*, N° III.) are to be had, by *their own Members*, on the Terms there fet down.

THESE are the General Defigns of this Society : and they have hitherto been enabled, by their own annual Subfcriptions, and the Legacies, or other cafual Benefactions of well difpofed Perfons, to raife a Fund fuffici nt to carry them on fuccefsfully, from Year to Year, at a very confiderable Expence : and they ftill truft to the Bleffing of G O D, and the Zeal of their Members, that fuch good Works will never fail to *flourifh* and *abound*, for lack of liberal Supplies from charitable Chriftians.

1710. BESIDE thefe general Defigns, the *Society* undertook, in the Year 1710, the Management of fuch Charities,

[7]

rities, as were, or fhould be, put into their Hands, for the Support and Enlargement of the PROTESTANT MISSION, then maintained by the King of *Denmark* at *Tranquebar* in the EAST-INDIES, for the Conver- fion of the Heathens, in thofe Parts. Accordingly, they, from Time to Time, affifted the Miffionaries there, with *Money*, a *Printing Prefs*, *Paper*, and other Ne- ceffaries, till the Year 1728; when, upon a Pro- pofal made by the Reverend Mr. *Schultz*, one of the *Danifh* Miffionaries, to remove to *Fort St. George*, and there begin a new Miffion, for the Converfion of the Heathens at *Madras*, the Society, trufting to the Goodnefs and Blefling of Almighty GOD, engaged for the Support of the fame, though at an Expence, that did then far exceed their Ability; which Expence has been fince greatly increafed, by an Addition of Miffionaries, as well as the Enlarge- ment of the Miffion to *Cudulore*, near *Fort St. David*, another *Englifh* Settlement; by the Erection of a Miffion and School at *Calcutta* in *Bengal*, for the Inftruction of Children in Writing, Reading, and the Principles of Chriftianity; and, lately, by the Eftablifhment of another Miffion, at *Tirutfchinapally*, the Capital of the Kingdom of *Madura*, an inland Country in *Eaft-India*; which has fince then been extended to *Tanjore*. However, the Society chear- fully rely upon the fame Wife and Gracious Provi- dence, which has hitherto wonderfully blefled this, and all their other Undertakings, to raife up fuch a true Chriftian Spirit, as will abundantly fupply all their Wants; fuch a Spirit, as fhewed itfelf in the late Reverend Mr. *Ziegenhagen*, *German* Chaplain to His Majefty, and the late Profeffors *Francke*, *Freyling- haufen*, and *Schultz* of *Hall* in *Saxony*. The prefent

(margin) Proteftant Miffion to Eaft-India, at Tranquebar. 1728. At Madras. 1737. At Cudulore. 1758. At Calcutta. 1766. Tirutfchina- pally.

fent State of this Miſſion may be feen in the *Appendix*, N° IV. together with an Account of the Benefactions received, at the End of N° V.

1720.   IN the Year 1720, the Society extended their Regard to the *Greek* Church in *Paleſtine*, *Syria*, *Meſopotamia*, *Arabia*, and *Egypt*. To this End, they publiſhed Propoſals for printing here, with a new Set

New Teſta- of Types, the *New Teſtament*, and *Pſalter*, in *Ara-*
ments, Pſal- *bick :* and were enabled, by the Bleſſing of GOD, on
ters, Cate- *chiſm, and* the Recommendation of the Biſhops, joined to the
Abridgment of Charity and Zeal of their own Members, to procure
the Hiſtory of an Edition of above 6000 *Pſalters*, and 10,000 *Teſta-*
the Bible, *ments*, as alſo of 5000 *Catechetical Inſtructions*, with
printed in *Arabick.* an *Abridgment of the Hiſtory of the Bible* annexed, at ſo large an Expence as the Sum of 2,976*l.* 1*s.* 6½*d.* ; to which His late Majeſty King *George* I. was a bountiful Contributor; by a gracious Benefaction of *Five Hundred Pounds.* 5,898 *Pſalters*, 4,246 *New Teſtaments*, and 2,248 *Catechetical Inſtructions*, with the *Abridgment* aforeſaid, have been already ſent to thoſe Parts ; into *Perſia*, by means of their Correſpondents, in *Ruſſia*; or into *India*, through the Hands of their Miſſionaries ; and the reſt are reſerved to be ſent, as Occaſion ſhall offer.

1725.   THE Society, having had the Pleaſure to ſee the Succeſs of the Endeavours uſed, in many Towns and Villages, for employing the Poor and their Children, by ſetting up WORKHOUSES, that nothing might be wanting to encourage the Proſecution of ſo uſeful a Deſign, they cauſed, in the Year 1725, a Collection of the beſt Accounts of ſuch

Workhouſes WORKHOUSES to be publiſhed ; which was reprinted,
recommend- with very large Additions, in 1733 ; in order to re-
ed. commend and forward, throughout the Kingdom, the

Execution

Execution of the fame Scheme, wherein a particular
Regard ought always to be had to fuch an Education
of poor Children, as may, by bringing them up in
the Faith, Knowledge, and Obedience of the Gofpel, prove, through the Grace of God, the moft ef-
fectual Means to make them ufeful Members of the
Community, as well as truly happy in the Life that
now is, and in that which is to come.

IN the Beginning of the Year 1732, the Society, 1732.
when they heard the melancholy Account of the Sufferings of the Proteftants in *Saltzburg*, having firft
obtained His Majefty's Leave, refolved upon doing
all that lay in their Power to raife Collections, for their *Saltzburg*
perfecuted Brethren. To this End, in *June* the fame *Exiles re-*
Year, they publifhed *An Account of the Sufferings of* *lieved.*
the perfecuted Proteftants in the Archbifhoprick of Saltzburg, *&c.* and afterwards publifhed *A further Account*
of their Sufferings, &c. with an *Extract of the Journals*
of M. Von Reck, *the Commiffary of the firft Tranfport*
of Saltzburgers *to* Georgia, *and of the Minifters that*
accompanied them thither, 1733. Thefe *Accounts*,
being enforced by the generous Example of many Noble and Honourable Perfons, as alfo by liberal Contributions, and earneft Exhortations from the Right
Reverend the Bifhops, and their Clergy, had, through
GOD's Bleffing, fo good an Effect upon the Minds of
charitable and well-difpofed Chriftians, of every Rank
and Denomination, that the Society, befides making
many large Remittances to *Germany*, were enabled to
fend over to the *Englifh* Colony in *Georgia*, in the
Years 1733, 1734, 1735, and 1741, four Tranfports,
confifting of more than two Hundred Proteftant Emi-
grants, chiefly *Saltzburgers*; who, with two Miffionaries and a School-mafter, fettled by themfelves, at

B   *Ebenezer*,

Ebenezer, upon such Lands, as were assigned to them, by the Trustees for establishing the said Colony.

THE great Expence of these Transports, and the many extraordinary Charges, that were necessary, for the Support and Encouragement of this Infant Settlement, together with 100 *l.* a Year, as a Salary for their Two Missionaries and School-master, had so far reduced the Charities, belonging to this Branch of the SOCIETY's Designs, that they had nothing left to answer any future Wants and Contingencies, excepting 2500 *l.* New South Sea Annuities, which had been purchased, as a standing Fund, for paying the aforesaid Annual Salary, to the Missionaries and School-master. But the lowering of public Interest so affected the *Society*, that they knew not how to make good this *Annual Salary*, towards which they continued to receive little or no Assistance. Being desirous, however, that this good Work should not fail for Want of Support, they, out of the Money raised by the Annual Subscriptions of their Members, and other Benefactions, purchased 833 *l.* 6 *s.* 8 *d.* New South Sea Annuities to be added to that Fund; trusting, that the good Providence of GOD, which hath hitherto wonderfully blessed all their Endeavours, would raise them up Benefactors to supply what might, on this Account, be wanting towards the several Branches of their charitable Designs.

THE Revolution in *America* occasioning a Separation between that Country, and this, and the Rev. Mr. *Triebner*, the Society's last Missionary at *Ebenezer*, having experienced many Difficulties and Hardships, in consequence of his Loyalty to the *British* Government, and being, at length, obliged to take Refuge in *England*, (where, in consequence

of the Society's Recommendation, he has been
kindly noticed by the Commissioners appointed to
examine the Claims of *American* Loyalists,) this
Mission is of course now discontinued; and the Funds
which the Society had appropriated towards its Support, will henceforth be applied to the General
Designs.

In the Year 1743, the Society undertook a new
Edition of the *Bible*, in the *Welch* Language, with the
Common Prayer, and *Pfalms* in *Metre :* and finished
it in 1748, by an Impreffion of *Fifteen Thoufand* Copies, which they difperfed in the moft prudent, ufeful,
and extenfive Manner they could. But, fuch was the
Zeal and Thirft of good Chriftians, throughout *Wales*,
for having the *Holy Scriptures* in that Language,
(wherein alone they could poffibly read them) that
this Impreffion, large as it was, fell exceedingly fhort
of the univerfal Demand, that was made for it. For
which Reafon, the Society, from a compaffionate and
Chriftian Regard to their Wants, put into the Prefs
another Edition of the Bible, confifting of the fame
Number of Copies ; as likewife of Five Thoufand
New Teftaments, and as many *Common Prayer Books*,
in the fame Language. This fecond Edition was alfo,
by the Bleffing of God, happily finifhed, and diftri-
buted; fince which Time, the Society, at the earneft
Defire of the Natives of *Wales*, undertook a Third
Edition of the *Old* and the *New Teftaments*, in a large
Octavo Size, with the Marginal References ; and
Twenty Thoufand Copies were printed, with a larger
Letter, than that which was ufed, in the former Editions. The Charge of this Impreffion was fo great,
that the Society, befides finking all the Fund, which
they had in Hand, towards that Defign, incurred a Debt

Propof. for Printing the Bible, &c. in the Welch Language. 1743.

1752.

1768.

B 2 of

cf above Two Thoufand Pounds, which however
has been difcharged, and a new Edition in 8vo. of
1799. *Ten Thoufand* Copies of the *Old* and *New Teftament*,
with Service and Pfalms, and *Two Thoufand* Copies
of the *New Teftament*, has been undertaken, and
printed, at the *Oxford* Prefs, in Confequence of
Reprefentations from their Lordfhips the Bifhops
of *Wales*, that another Edition was wanted. The
Charge of this Edition, the SOCIETY has undertaken from its general Funds, and mean to difpofe
of it, in the Principality, at one Half of the prime
Coft in Sheets.

Truft for the Benefit of the Scilly Iflands. IN the Year 1752, the Society accepted a Truft
from the Rev. Mr. *Hartfhorne*, Rector of *Brofely*, Sa-
1752. *lop*, who, commiferating the fpiritual Wants of the
Off-Iflands of *Scilly*, made them an Offer of 200 *l.*
towards fending a Deacon to *Trefco*, together with
50 *l.* towards erecting a Library, for his Ufe. But, that
Sum being inadequate to the Purpofe, nothing was
Schools o- pened. done in this Bufinefs till the Year 1765, when, de-
1765. viating a little from the original Plan, they opened
Schools, in each of the Off-Iflands. Senfible, however,
that this was, by no Means, a fufficient Provifion for
the religious Inftruction of the Inhabitants, the Society
have fince refumed the former Plan, and having pub-
Propofals for fending a Miffiner to the Iflands. lifhed an Account of the State of Religion, in thofe
Iflands, they received fuch Encouragement and Affift-
1774. ance, that they carried their pious and charitable
Purpofe into Execution. They appointed the Rev.
Mr. *Coxon* to this Miffion; but his infirm State of
Health would not permit him to continue long, in the
Service of the Society. They afterwards engaged the
Rev. Mr. *John Troutbeck* as their Miffionary, who
was removed from *Trefco*, to St. *Mary's*. The Rev.
Mr.

Mr. *William Davies* was recommended to the Society, as a proper Person to succeed Mr. *Troutbeck*; on whose Removal, in the Year 1796, the Rev. *David Evans*, M.A. was appointed to the Mission at *Tresco*. And in the Year 1797, the Rev. *William Croker*, B.A. was appointed to the Cure of St. *Agnes* Island. See *Appendix*, N° IV.

In the Year 1763, the Society gave out Proposals for printing Bibles, Common Prayers, and other Religious Books, in the Vulgar Tongue of the *Isle of Mann*; and, by the Encouragement they met with, were enabled to print and disperse, *gratis*, among the Inhabitants 2000 *Church Catechisms*, 1200 *Christian Monitors*, 2000 *Lewis's Expositions*, 1000 Copies of the *New Testament* in Octavo, 1550 *Common Prayers* in the same Size, and 1000 in Twelves. They have likewise printed 2000 Copies of the *Old Testament* in Octavo, together with the like Number of the *New*, the former Impression not having been by any Means sufficient to answer the Demands of the People; and intend to proceed in this charitable Work, and to supply the *Isle of Mann* with other good Books and Tracts, or with new Editions of such as have been already published for their Use. See *Appendix*, N° IV.

margin: Proposal for Printing the Bible, &c. in the Manks Language. 1763.

BEFORE we conclude this *general* Account, it may not be improper to mention some very considerable and standing Benefactions to this Society.

1. THE first is a most generous *Legacy* of *Four Thousand Pounds*, which was left to them by Mrs. *Elizabeth Palmer*, in 1728, and is still preserved entire in the *Public Funds*; viz. 2800 *l.* in New South Sea Annuities, and 1200 *l.* in South Sea Stock, the Interest of it only being, from Year to Year, applied to such Branches of their Designs, as most need it.

margin: Mrs. *Palmer's* Legacy of 4000 *l.* in 1728.

2. THE

2. THE fecond is a free Gift in the Year 1734, by Mr. *Edwin Belke*, a Gentleman of *Kent*, deceafed ; who left to the Society Ten Acres of Land in *Romney Marſh*, in *Kent*, now let at 10 *l. per Annum*, free of all Taxes and other Deductions ; and likewife 1050 *l.* New South Sea Annuities, towards defraying the Expence of diſtributing, gratis, *Bibles, New Teſtaments*, and other Religious Books, under the Infpection of the Society.

THE fame Gentleman did alfo, in the Year 1737, give the Society *Eighty Pounds* New South Sea Annuities ; the Dividends whereof are to be laid out, from Time to Time, (at the Direction of the Society) in Books for propagating the Chriſtian Religion in the *Eaſt-Indies*, or other Parts of the World.

3. THE next is a Legacy of the Reverend Doctor *Thomas Carter*, formerly Vice-Provoſt of *Eton*, whofe Executors (befides the Payment of 436 *l.* 3 *s.* 9½ *d.* in Money) transferred to the Society 295 *l.* 5 *s.* 11 *d.* in New South Sea Annuities, and 110 *l.* in Bank Stock. The former of thefe Articles has been fince made up 300 *l.* and the latter 200 *l.* for a Fund to anfwer, by the annual Intereſt thereof, the Ufes directed by the Teſtator's Will, particularly that of printing or publiſhing, in the *Eaſtern* Languages, *Bibles, Old* and *New Teſtaments*, or what Part thereof the Society ſhall judge proper.

4. The fourth is a Legacy of *Samuel Percivall*, Efq; of *Pendarves*, in *Cornwall*, of 1000 *l.* which was bequeathed to the Reverend Dr. *William Stackhoufe*, and Mr. *James Dunn, in Truſt only and for the entire Benefit of promoting the Propagation of Chriſtian Knowledge in foreign Parts :* Which Sum, the faid Truſtees paid to the Society, on the above-mentioned

ed Truſt; and they have appropriated it to the Support of the Proteſtant Miſſion, in the *Eaſt-Indies*.

5. The fifth is a generous Benefaction of 600*l*. 1762. from an unknown Hand, by the Secretary, which, according to the Direction of the Donor, has been laid out in the Purchaſe of 700 *l*. New South Sea Annuities, and added to the Fund for the Support of the *Eaſt-India Miſſion:*

6. In the Year 1775, the Right Rev. *John*, Lord 1775. Biſhop of *Wincheſter*, and the Rev. *William Buller*, (now Lord Biſhop of *Exeter*) as Executors of the late Mrs. *Ann Maynard*, Spinſter, having a Sum of Money to diſpoſe of, in ſuch Ways, as they judged moſt likely to promote the Glory of God, and the Welfare of Mankind, gave to the Society the Sum of 300*l*. towards the Support of the *Scilly* Miſſion.

7. In the Year 1786, the Rt. Hon Lady *Godolphin*, 1786. as Executrix of the late Lord *Godolphin*, paid the Sum of 2000*l*. being his Lordſhip's Legacy, to be applied towards carrying on the Deſigns of the Society; which, by Direction of the Board, has been laid out in the Purchaſe of 2700*l*. 3 per Cent. Conſols.

8. And in the Year 1791, *Peter Huguetan Van Vryhouven*, Lord of *Vryheuven*, in the Province of 1791. *Holland*, died at *London*, bequeathing to the Society, by his laſt Will, after the Payment of many other very conſiderable Legacies, two-thirds of the Reſidue of his perſonal Property. The Particulars of this important Will being ſubmitted by the Executors to the Direction of the Court of Chancery, the Court made a final Decree in the Buſineſs, in the Year 1796, when Property in ſeveral of the public Funds was transferred to the Society's three Treaſurers, in Truſt for the *General Deſigns* of the Society,

Society, which together yields Dividends amounting to nearly 3,300*l. per Ann.*

THESE are the *general* Defigns wherein the Society are at prefent engaged; the *particular* State whereof will be publifhed every Year; and what it now is, together with their Receipts and Difburfements from the former Audit, 22 *March*, 1798, to the laft Audit, 29 *March*, 1799, may be feen in the *Appendix*, N° V.

The TREASURERS of this SOCIETY.

ROBERT POOLE FINCH, D.D. Prebendary of *Weſtmin-ſter*, is Treaſurer for all Benefactions to the Deſigns of the SOCIETY in general.

HENRY HUGH HOARE, Eſq. Banker, in *Fleet-Street*, is Treaſurer to the *Proteſtant Miſſion*, in the *Eaſt-Indies*.

FRANCIS GOSLING, Eſq; Banker, in *Fleet-Street*, is Treaſurer for all *Annual Subſcriptions*, and alſo for all *Remittances* for *Packets* of Books ſent to any Members.

GEORGE GASKIN, D.D. is Secretary to the Society.

Mr. JOHN ROBINSON, Clerk and Collector.

All Letters, on the Society's Buſineſs, are to be directed to the Reverend Dr. Gaſkin, *at the Society's Houſe, in* Bartlett's Buildings, Holborn.

It is hereby deſired of all Members of the Society, or other Perſons, who have any Buſineſs with the SECRETARY or CLERK, that they would come, or ſend to the Society's Houſe, in *Bartlett's Buildings, Holborn,* between *Nine* in the Morning and *Two* in the Afternoon, within which Hours Attendance is given in the Office every Week-Day, excepting *Saturday*.

N. B. *Tueſday* is the only Day, whereon (according to the Standing Orders of the Society) their Committee meet to give Directions for anſwering the Letters received, and for ordering Books to be ſent, that may be requeſted on the Terms of the Society.

C   THE

R U L E S and O R D E R S

OF THE

S O C I E T Y

FOR PROMOTING

CHRISTIAN KNOWLEDGE.

Orders relating to the SOCIETY *in general.*

I. THAT this SOCIETY be called by the Name
of **The Society for Promoting Christian
Knowledge**: and that they meet the firſt *Tueſday* in
every Month, at Eleven of the Clock in the Forenoon, and enter upon Buſineſs preciſely at Twelve.

II. THAT no Buſineſs ſhall commence, till the
Devotions annexed to theſe ſtanding Rules are per-
formed; and that nothing be concluded on, till four
of the ſubſcribing Members are preſent; but in caſe
that Number ſhould not attend, that then the Members preſent act as a Committee.

III. THAT the Chair be filled Monthly by a
Choice of one of the Members preſent, and that at
each Monthly Meeting a Chairman ſhall be declared,
who ſhall preſide (except when a Biſhop is preſent)
at every Meeting of the Committee, during his
Month; but in his Abſence, his Place may be ſupplied by ſuch Member, as the Society, or Committee, ſhall agree upon for that Day.

IV. THAT

IV. THAT at every Meeting of the Society, the
Minutes of the foregoing Meeting, and the Minutes
of the intervening Committees, be read; all new
Motions and Reports be made; and such Letters,
or Abſtracts of them, be read, as the Committee
ſhall direct to be laid before the Society.

V. THAT when any Perſon, (excepting a Biſhop)
living within the Bills of Mortality, is propoſed,
either for a Subſcribing or Correſponding Member,
he ſhall be recommended by two Members at leaſt,
who ſhall certify his Qualifications, in the following
Form, with the Year and Day of the Month, and
their Names ſignified underneath.

" WE the Underwritten do recommend A. B.
" to be a Member of the SOCIETY
" for Promoting Chriſtian Knowledge, and do verily
" believe that he is well affected to His Majeſty
" King GEORGE, and his Government, and to the
" Church of England as by Law eſtabliſhed; of a
" ſober and religious Life and Converſation; and of
" an humble, peaceable, and charitable Diſpoſition."

But if the Perſon propoſed live at a greater Diſtance from London, it is ſufficient that he be ſo recommended by one Correſponding or Subſcribing
Member. That every Propoſal, thus ſigned, ſhall
be read to the Members preſent at that Meeting of
the Society, or Committee, (wherein ſuch Perſon
is firſt propoſed) who ſhall be deſired to inform themſelves about the Truth of the ſame: and that this
be done in like Manner at that Meeting of the ſaid
Society, when the Members preſent proceed to
Election. But, no Election ſhall be proceeded to,

until

until the Names of the Perfons propofed to be Members fhall have been hanging up in the Committee-Room of the Society, three Committee-Days at leaft, or on one previous Day of General Meeting.

VI. THAT the Election of all Members (excepting Bifhops) be made by Balloting ; and if there fhall be one fifth Part of the Members prefent diffentient, the Election fhall not be deemed valid.

VII. THAT the Determination of fuch Queftions as the Society cannot otherwife decide, be made by Balloting of the Subfcribing Members only ; and that when the Numbers in Balloting are equal, the Chairman fhall have the cafting Vote. N. B. Correfponding Members are defired to attend.

VIII. THAT no Perfon, chofen to be a Subfcribing Member, be confidered as fuch till he fignifies his Acceptance, by paying a Sum (not lefs than one Guinea) to the Treafurer for the Time being ; and by fubfcribing the fame Sum, or more, annually, for carrying on the Defigns of the Society ; unlefs he give twenty Pounds at or before his Admiffion as a Member.

IX. THAT any Correfponding Member, who fhall afterward fubfcribe a yearly Sum of one Guinea, or more, to the Defigns of the Society, fhall be deemed a Subfcribing Member, without any new Election.

X. THAT no Sum exceeding forty Shillings be difpofed of, (excepting for Books ordered upon the Terms of the Society) without confidering the State of the Society's Cafh : and that the Society do not enter into any new Article of Expence, which may occafion a Charge of twenty Pounds, or upwards, without giving Notice thereof in the printed Summons,

(which

(which are to be always fent out before the Meetings of the Society) to the Subfcribing Members in,
and about, *London*.

XI. T H A T the Society will always decline the
intermeddling with fuch Matters, as are foreign to
their Defign of *Promoting Chriftian Knowledge*.

XII. T H A T the Society have an Anniverfary
Meeting of their Members, to dine together once
every Year: and that the Day be fixed when the
Report of the Auuit is made.

XIII. T H A T none of the *ftanding Orders* be re-
pealed, fufpended, or altered, till fuch Repeal, Suf-
penfion, or Alteration, has been propofed at two
fucceffive Meetings of the Committee ; and not determined till the next Meeting of the Society, when
there fhall be at leaft ten of the Subfcribing Members
prefent; and that the fame Rule be obferved for
revoking, or altering, any thing, that has been fettled
by Balloting.

XIV. T H A T no Member of the Society, or any
other Perfon, be at Liberty to tranfcribe, or take a
Copy of any Minute of the Proceedings of the Society, or of any Letter or Papers, fent to the Society, without the Confent of the Board.

XV. T H A T no Perfon be an Officer of the Society, who is not a Member of the Church of *England*, as by Law eftablifhed : and that whenever any
Vacancy fhall happen, the Board fhall not proceed
to admit any Perfon to be a Candidate, till they have
firft fatisfied themfelves, that he is qualified as above
directed.

XVI. T H A T it be recommended to every Member
to pray to Almighty G O D for a Bleffing on the Con-
fultations, and Endeavours, of the Society.

XVII. T H A T

XVII. THAT when any Member is indifpofed, and defires the Prayers of the Society, the Colleƈt, or Colleƈts, ufed in the Office for vifiting the Sick, be added to their ufual Form.

Orders relating to the General Committee.

I. THAT a General Committee of the Society's Members meet Weekly, on *Tuefday* Morning, by Eleven of the Clock ; that Prayers be faid, and Bufinefs be entered upon, precifely at Twelve ; and that the faid Committee confift of three, at leaft, of the Subfcribing Members.

II. THAT they confider all References to them from the Society, and have Power to appoint Special Committees, and receive Reports from them, as alfo from the Committee for Receipts and Payments, or the Secretary : and that no Special Committee tranfaƈt any Bufinefs, but what is referred to them by the Society, or the General Committee.

III. THAT they have Power to difpatch all Bufinefs not particularly referved to the Society by their ftanding Orders.

IV. THAT the Committee make a Report of their Proceedings, at each Meeting of the Society : and that they, or any of their Treafurers, have Power to call an extraordinary Meeting of the Society, during the Interval of the ftated Monthly Meetings, as Occafion fhall require.

V. THAT the Letters to the Society may be read when two Subfcribing Members only are prefent, who fhall have Power to give Direƈtions for anfwering them, and for fending any Packet that fhall be defired, conformable to the Rules of the Society.

Orders relating to the Committee for Receipts and Payments.

I. THAT the feveral Treafurers of this Society, for the Time being, be the Committee for Receipts and Payments : and that they keep diftinct Accounts of all Subfcriptions, Benefactions, and Receipts of any kind; and of their Difburfements on the Society's Account.

II. THAT their Accounts be audited every Year, within one Month before, or after *Lady-Day*, by fuch Perfons, and on fuch Day, as the Society fhall appoint. And that the State of fuch Accounts, with a Lift of all Arrears then due, be laid before the Society, upon the Report of fuch Audit.

Orders relating to Books.

I. THAT a printed Lift be kept of all the So-ciety's Books and Papers, with the Prices, at which they are difpofed of, to their Members.

II. THAT no Manufcript be printed, nor any printed Book or Paper bought, or reprinted, or re-commended to the Society to be put into their Lift of Books, which are difperfed cccafionally among the Members upon the Terms of the Society, but fuch as fhall have been firft approved in manner fol-lowing ; that is to fay,

Every fuch Manufcript, printed Book, or Paper, fhall be recommended to the Society by three Sub-fcribing Members, who have read the fame ; and fhall report it proper and requifite to promote the Defigns of the Society : after which, every fuch

Manufcript,

Manuscript, printed Book, or Paper, shall be referred to four other Members, who are to report
their Opinion thereof, as soon as may be: and at
the next General Meeting after their Report, it shall
be determined by Balloting, whether such Book, or
Paper, shall be admitted into the said List.

III. THAT if any Book, or Paper, approved of
in manner aforesaid, shall be altered, or receive any
Additions, such Book, or Paper, shall not be dif-
persed by the Society, till such Alterations or Additions shall have been considered and approved of by
four Members, and pass a Ballot, in like manner as
before.

IV. THAT no Book, or Paper, received by the
Society, of which they have the Property, be reprinted without a new Order.

V. THAT any Book, or Paper, read, examined,
and approved by the Committee, and afterwards
agreed to by the Society, may be printed and dif-
persed, as the Society shall think fit, without passing
the Forms abovementioned.

VI. THAT the Sermon preached at the Anniversary Meeting of the Children educated in the Charity-
Schools, with the Account of the said Schools, and
the Abstract of the Society's Proceedings; and the
Sermon at the Anniversary Meeting of *The Society
for the Propagation of the Gospel in Foreign Parts,*
with the Abstract of their Proceedings, may be dif-
persed, without such Perusal and Examination as
aforesaid, provided the Committee shall approve of
the same.

Orders relating to Packets.

I. THAT to every new Subfcribing and Correfponding Member, be fent a Copy of the
printed Account of the Society, and of the ftanding
Rules and Orders, to inform them of its Conftitution and Defigns.

II. THAT any Subfcribing or Correfponding
Member, defiring a Packet of the Society's Books,
may be furnifhed with the fame, according to the
Regulation agreed upon *Anno* 1720, viz. The bound
Books at prime Coft in Quires, the Society being at
the Charge of Binding; and the Stitched Books at
half Price.

III. THAT no Book or Paper be, at any Time,
put into the Society's Packet, but by Confent of the
Society or their Committee.

Orders relating to the Secretary.

I. THAT the Secretary keep a fair Copy of the
Proceedings of the Society and Committees,
in a Book or Books for that Purpofe.

II. THAT he do make an Abftract of all Letters
fent from the Society, and enter the fame in a Book,
or Books, to be kept for that Purpofe: and alfo
enter into another Book, Copies at large of fuch
circular Letters as are fent to all the Members, and
of fuch other Letters, or Papers, as the Society, or
Committee, fhall direct.

III. THAT there be Indexes kept in diftinct
Books, viz. one of *Names* in the Abftract of Letters,
and another of *Things* contained in the Minutes.

D   IV. THAT

IV. THAT all Letters, on Account of the Society, be directed to their Secretary for the Time being; and by him brought to them, or the Committee.

V. THAT he do lay before the Chairman, at every Meeting of the Society, or Committee, a Copy of their *standing Orders*.

VI. THAT he likewise lay before them, at every such Meeting, an Account of what Business remains undetermined.

VII. THAT all the Orders of the Society for Books, to be furnished by their Bookseller for the Members, or other extraordinary Services, be signed by the Secretary, and returned by the Bookseller to the Society's Office, as his Vouchers, at the Audit.

VIII. THAT when the Society have approved of any Book to be distributed, and a Price is settled upon the same, the Secretary give Notice thereof to the Members in the Country, when they are occasionally written unto.

IX. THAT he do give Notice to every Subscribing and Corresponding Member, of his being elected; and that in his Letter of Notice to Subscribing Members, he do always transmit the seventh Order, relating to the Society in general.

X. THAT he once a Quarter lay before the Society a List of such as have been chosen Subscribing Members, but have not paid their Benefactions.

XI. THAT he do, after every Audit, enter fair into their Books, the several separate Accounts relating to

The Designs of the Society in general.

The Protestant Mission in the *East-Indies*.

Mr. *Belke's* Benefactions.

The Arabick Impression, &c. &c.

6 XII. THAT

XII. THAT he do, at the Anniverſary Meeting of the Society, lay before them an Abſtract of the moſt material Tranſactions of the preceding Year.

Orders relating to the Clerk, Meſſenger, and Collector.

I. THAT he do give Timely Notice of every Meeting of the Society, to the Subſcribing and Correſponding Members in, and about, *London*.

II. THAT he do attend all Meetings of the Society and Committees, to receive Orders and Directions.

III. THAT he do attend, in the Office, from Nine in the Morning till Two in the Afternoon, every Day, excepting *Saturday* and *Sunday*, to diſpatch the neceſſary Buſineſs of his Offices.

IV. THAT he give no Orders to the Bookſeller, or Printer, or contract any Debts with the Society's Tradeſmen, without an Order from the Board, or Leave from the Secretary.

V. THAT a Book of Packets, ſent to the Members, be kept ready to be laid before the Chairman, at every Meeting, wherein ſhall be entered the Day when each Packet was ordered, and when, and how, ſent, and the Value of it.

VI. THAT he do pay to the Treaſurer for Subſcriptions, whatever he receives on that Account, or for Arrears of Packets, as often as he ſhall have the Sum of 30 *l.* in his Hands.

VII. THAT on every *Tueſday*, he do pay to the Bookſeller whatever he receives for Packets in the Courſe of the preceding Week.

D 2   VIII. That

VIII. That he have ready to lay before the Board, the firſt *Tueſday,* in every Month, the ſeveral Books, wherein he keeps an Account of Bills ſent out of the Country, and of Money received for Subſcriptions, Benefactions, and Packets.

IX. THAT when any annual Subſcribing Member of this Society ſhall be one yearly Payment in Arrear, he be informed of the ſame, by a reſpectful Meſſage, or Letter, from this Society, to be ſent within three Months after ſuch Subſcription ſhall become due, if in *London,* or *Weſtminſter,* or within ten. Miles thereof; and if at a greater Diſtance, then ſuch Letter to be ſent within ſix Months after the Subſcription ſhall have become due.

X. That he do take care of the Books and Things that are in the Society's Store-Room, and keep an Account of what is delivered out by Order of the Society.

XI. THAT he do, once a Year, as ſoon as may be after the annual Account of the Society's Proceedings is printed, convey to all the Subſcribing Members in and about *London,* the Anniverſary Sermon, and Account of the Society, and likewiſe ſuch Tracts as ſhall be ordered by the Board; and that he alſo ſend the ſame to all Subſcribing, and Correſponding, Members in the Country.

APPEN-

A P P E N D I X.

N° I.

The Form of recommending MEMBERS, *according to the* Standing Orders *of the* SOCIETY.

WE the Underwritten do recommend *A. B.* to be a   Member of THE SOCIETY FOR PROMOTING CHRISTIAN KNOWLEDGE; and do verily believe that He is well affected to His Majefty King GEORGE, and his Government; and to the Church of *England*, as by Law eftablifhed; of a fober and religious Life and Converfation, and of an humble, peaceable, and charitable Difpofition.

A

L I S T

OF THE

SUBSCRIBING MEMBERS

OF THE

SOCIETY for PROMOTING CHRISTIAN KNOWLEDGE.

Time of
Admiffion.

1790 His Royal Highness George, Prince of Wales.

A.

1777 RIGHT Rev. *Lewis*, Lord Bifhop of St. *Afaph.*

1765 Mr. *Thomas Adderley, Doctors-Commons, London.*

1769 Rev. *Townfend Andrews*, LL.B. Prebendary of St. *Paul's.*

1775 *Nicholas Baptift Aubert*, Efq; *Hackney.*

1779 Rev. *Eaft Apthorp*, D.D. Prebendary of *Finfbury.*

1781 General *G. Ainflie, Devonfhire Place, London.*

1783 *Paul Agutter*, Efq; *Aldermanbury, London.*

1784 Rev. *Robert Afhe*, D.D. of *Crewkerne, Somerfetfhire.*

1785 *Hugh Ackland*, Efq; *Exmouth, Devon.*

1786 Mr. *Thomas Atkinfon, Huddersfield, Yorkfhire.*

John

1786 *John Hiley Addington*, Efq; *Old Palace Yard*.
1787 Rev. *T. Ackland*, M. A. Rector of *Chrift-church, Surry*.
Rev. *John Alcock*, M.A. Vicar General of *Raphoe*.
1788 Rev. *Richard Atlay*, M. A. Head Mafter of the Free
Grammar School, in *Stamford*.
1789 Rev. *John Argles*, LL.B. *Tenterden, Kent*.
Stephen Aifley, Efq; *Kenfington, Middlefex*.
Rev. *John Amphlett*, D. D. *Dodderhill, Worcefterfhire*.
1790 Rev. *J. Afhpinfhaw*, M.A. Rector of *St. Peter's, Nottingh*.
Captain *Armftrong*, of *Percy-ftreet*.
1791 *William Thornton Aftell*, Efq; of *Clapham*.
Rev. *C. Alderfon*, LL.B. Rector of *Eckington, Derbyfh*.
Rev. *G. Andrewes*, M.A. Rect. of *Zeal-Monachorum, Devon*.
Rev. *Geo. Anderfon*, M.A. Vicar of *Cranfley, Northampt*.
Hon. Sir *William Henry Afhhurft*, Knt.
1793 Rev. *Wm. Agutter*, M.A. Chaplain at the *Afylum*.
1794 Rev. *Wm. Antrobus*, B.D. Rect. of *St. Andrew Underfhaft*.
Rev. *Geo. Anguifh*, M. A. Prebendary of *Norwich*.
Rev. *Geo. Allanfon*, M. A. Rector of *Malpas, Chefhire*.
1795 *Tho. Apperley*, Efq; *Plâs Gronnow*, near *Wrexham, Denb*.
Rev. *R Aldridge*, Vicar of *North Petherton, Somerfetfhire*
Rev. *John Andrew*, Rector of *Powderham, Devon*.
1797 Rev. *Wm. Alingtou*, B.A. *Gravely, Herts*.
Jafper Atkinfon, Efq; *Aldermanbury*.
1798 *Adam Afkew*, Efq; *Wimpole-ftreet*.
John P. Anderdon, Efq; *Highbury Grove, Iflington*.
1799 *John Ackland*, Efq; *Fairfield Houfe*, near *Bridgwater*.
Rev. *John Adey Anftis*, Vicar of *Betton, Glocefterfhire*.
George Arnold, Efq; *Halftead Place, Kent*.
Rev. *Jofeph Alderfon*, M.A. Rector of *Hexingham, Norf*.
Mr. *John Allen*, *Whitechapel-road*.

B.

1751 **R**Ight Rev. *Charles*, Lord Bifhop of *Bath* and *Wells*.
1755 Right Rev. *John*, Lord Bifhop of *Bangor*.

Right

1798 Right Rev. *Foiliott*, Lord Bifhop of *Briflol*.
1796 Right Hon. Lord *Belgrave*.
1752 Rev. *John Blyth*, Vicar of *Colefhill*, *Warwickfhire*.
    Rev. *Brook Bridges*, M. A. *Caftle Hedningham*, *Effex*.
1753 Rev. *Samuel Baker*, Rector of *Kirby-Cane*, *Norfolk*.
1760 Rev. *Richard Bullock*, D. D. Rector of *Stretham*, *Surry*,
    and St. *Paul*, *Covent-Garden*.
    Jonathan Blundell, Efq; Merchant in *Liverpool*.
1764 Rev. *William Browne*, M. A. Rector of *Thorley*, *Herts*.
1766 Rev. *Walter Bagot*, M. A. Rector of *Blyfield*, *Staffordfh*.
1767 Rev. *Tho. Bedford*, Rector of *Philleigh*, *Cornwall*.
    Rev. *Cha. Blackftone*, LL.B. Fellow of *Winton* College.
1768 *John Peploe Birch*, Efq; *Garnftone*, *Herefordfhire*.
1769 *John Bowman*, Efq; *Craike*, *Durham*.
    Rev. *Sam. Barwick*, Rector of *Burton Latimer*, *Northamp*.
1770 Rev. *Samuel Bulkely*, M. A. *Hatfield*, *Herts*.
    Rev. *Ric. Brereton*, M.A. Rector of *Edgworth*, *Glocefterfh*.
    Henry Bell, Efq; *Worlington*, *Norfolk*.
1771 *Philip Bowes Broke*, Efq; *Nacton*, *Suffolk*.
    Rev. *Tho. Boyce*, M. A. *Great Waldingfield*, *Sudbury*.
1772 Rev. *William Blencowe*, M. A. Canon of *Wells*.
1773 *Thomas Berney Bramflon*, Efq; M.P. of *Skreens*, *Effex*.
    Rev. *Thomas Bowman*, Prebendary of *Lincoln*, and
    Rector of *Craike*, *Durham*.
    Robert Carr Brackenbury, Efq; of *Spilfby*, *Lincolnfhire*.
1774 *Bryan Broughton*, Efq; of the Treafury.
1775 Rev. *James Bayley*, M. A. Fellow of *Manchefter* College.
1776 *William Banks*, Efq; *Winflanley*, *Lancafhire*.
    Rev. *Roger Burt*, M. A. Rector of *Odcombe*, *Somerfet*.
1777 Rev. —— *Bouyer*, Rector of *Willoughby*, *Lincolnfhire*.
    Mr. *John Bode*, of the General Poft-Office.
    Rev. *John Brock*, *Much Eaflon*, *Effex*.
    Rev. *Henry Bathurft*, LL.D. Prebendary of *Durham*.
    John Baker, Efq; *Princes-flreet*, *Spitalfields*.
Rev.

1778 Rev. *William Bell*, D.D. Prebendary of *Weſtminſter*.
      Sam. Blencowe, Eſq; *Marſton St. Lawrence, Northamp.*
1779 Rev. *Ric. Budworth*, M. A. Rector of *High Laver, Eſſex.*
      Richard Burfoot, Eſq; *Lambeth.*
1780 Rev. *Wm. Baynes*, M. A. Rector of *Rickinghall, Suffolk.*
1781 Mr. *Thomas Baſkerfeild*, Sen. *Hart-ſtreet, Bloomſbury.*
      Rev. *Edw. Baynes*, M. A. Rector of *St. Mary Week, Corn.*
      Rev. *Wm. B. Barter*, M. A. Rector of *Timſbury, Bath.*
      Rev. *Ant. Bliſſe*, A. B. Vicar of *Meridan, Warwickſhire.*
      Rev. *Reginald Brathwaite*, M. A. *Hawkeſhead, Lancaſhire.*
      Rev. *Edward Bowerbank*, B. D. Rector of *Croft, Yorkſh.*
      Rev. *Wm. Lloyd Baker*, M. A. *Stout's Hill, Glouceſterſh.*
1782 *John Bacon*, Eſq; Firſt-Fruits Office, *Temple.*
      Rev. *John Benſon*, D. D. Prebendary of *Canterbury.*
      Rev. *Rowland Berkeley*, LL. D. Vicar of *Writtle, Eſſex.*
      Rev. *John Buxton*, Rector of *Carleton Rode, Norfolk.*
      Rev. *Andrew Burnaby*, D. D. Archdeacon of *Leiceſter.*
1783 Rev. *Henry Blacket*, M. A. Rector of *Boldon, Durham.*
      Rev. *Tho. Bateman*, M. A. Vicar of *Whaplode, Lincolnſh.*
1784 Sir *Tho. Crawley Bovey*, Bart. *Flaxly-Abbey, Glouceſterſh.*
      Rev. *Slade Baker*, LL. B. Rector of *Buſcot, Berkſhire.*
      Rev. *Wm. Baker*, LL. B. Rector of *Dowdeſwell, Glouceſt.*
      Mr. *James Brant, Cheapſide.*
1785 Rev. *F. Barnes*, D. D. Maſter of *St. Peter's* Coll. *Camb.*
      Rev. *Jonathan Boucher*, M. A. Vicar of *Epſom, Surry.*
      Rev. *Edw. Brackenbury, Skendleby, Lincolnſhire.*
      Rev. *Philip Bell*, M. A. Vicar of *Stow-Bardolph, Norfolk.*
      Mr. *John Bullen, Morgan's Lane, Southwark.*
      Mr. *Thomas Baſkerfeild*, Jun. *Hart-ſtreet, Bloomſbury.*
      Rev. *John Charles Beckingham*, LL. B. Rector of *Upper
        Hardres, Kent.*
      Rev. *Thomas Beynon*, Prebendary of *Brecon*, and Rector
        of *Penboyr, Carmarthenſhire.*
1786 Rev. *Tho. Blyth*, M. A. Rector of *Elmdon, Warwickſh.*

1786 Rev. *Thomas Blackburne, Thelwall, Chefhire.*
Rev. *Geo. Barrington,* M. A. Rector of *Sedgefield, Durh.*
Rev. *Tho. Burgefs,* B. D. Prebendary of *Durham.*
Mr. *John Brickwood,* of *Lime-ftreet.*
Thomas B. Bayley, Efq; *Hope,* near *Manchefter.*
C. R. Broughton, Efq; of the *Secretary of State's Office.*
1787 Rev. *John Bell,* D. D. Chaplain to the Factory at
    Oporto, and Fellow of St. *John's* College, *Oxford.*
Thomas Babington, Efq; *Rothley Temple, Leicefterfh.*
Anthony Brough, Efq; *Clapham.*
Rev. *Martin Benfon,* M. A. Rector of *Meeftham, Surry.*
Rev. *Henry Beauclerk,* Rector of *Whittlebury, Northamp.*
Rev. *Wm. Buckle,* M. A. Vicar of *Pyrton, Oxfordfhire.*
Rev. *Tho. Bentham,* M. A. Rector of *Woodnorton, Norfolk.*
Rev. *Tho. W. Barlow,* M. A. Prebendary of *Briftol.*
Rev. *Gilb. Burrington,* M. A. Vicar of *Chudleigh, Devon.*
Leonard Bartholomew, Efq; *Addington-place, Kent.*
William Bullock, Efq; *Little Burfted, Effex.*
Rev. *Cha. Barton,* M.A. Rector of St. *Andrew's, Holborn.*
Rev. *Ralph Bridge,* M. A. *Malpas, Chefhire.*
Rev. *Henry Burton,* Vicar of *Atcham, Shropfhire.*
John Thompfon Bull, Efq; *Great Burfted, Effex.*
Rev. *George Boulton,* M. A. Rector of *Great Oxendon,*
    and Vicar of *Sutton cum Wefton, Northamptonfhire.*
Rev. *Wm. Butts,* B.D. Rector of *Little Wilbraham, Camb.*
Rev. *Ric. F. Belward,* D.D. Mafter of *Caius Coll. Camb.*
1788 Rev. *Tho. Biker,* M. A. Vicar of *Culworth, Northamp.*
Walter Biunt, Efq; *Wallop, Hants.*
Alexander Bennett, Efq; Exchequer Office, *Temple.*
Mr. *Peter Barnett, Birmingham.*
Rev. *Cha. Wm. Burrell,* M.A. Fellow of *Cath.* Hall, *Camb.*
Rev. *John Bruton,* Vicar of *Cullumpton, Devon.*
Rev. *George Beever,* M. A. Rector of *North Cove, cum*
    Willingham, Norfolk.

                                Rev.

1788 Rev. *George Bingham*, B.D. Rector of *Pimpern, Dorset*.
Rev. *John Bishop*, D.D. Rector of *Mells*, near *Frome, Somerf*.
1789 Mr. *Brook Bridges, Red Lion-fquare*.
Rev. *Rob. C. Blayney*, M.A. Rector of *Pisford, Northamp*.
Rev. *Benjamin Blayney*, D.D. Regius Profeffor of He-
brew, and Canon of *Chrift Church, Oxford*.
Rev. *William Borlafe*, M.A. Vicar of *Madrom, Cornwall*.
Mr. *Samuel Birch, Cornhill, London*.
Charles Berners, Efq; *Woolverfton Hall*, near *Ipfwich*.
Rev. *Wm. Butts*, M.A. Rector of *Glemsford, Suffolk*.
Mr. *Thomas Birch, Queen's-College, Oxford*.
1790 Mr. *Thomas Breach, Bond-ftreet*.
Rev. *W. Beloe*, M.A. Rector of *Alhallows, London Wall*.
Rev. *Sackville S. Bale*, M.A. Rector of *Withyham, Suffex*.
Rev. *Fred. W. Blomberg*, M.A. Prebendary of *Briftol*.
George Briftow, Efq; *Merchant Taylors'-Hall*.
Rev. *George Bridgman*, Rector of *Wigan*.
1791 Rev. *Thomas Booth*, M.A. Vicar of *Spilfby, Lincolnfhire*.
Rev. *Thomas Bracken*, M.A. Clerk in Orders of *St.
James's, Weftminfter*.
Rev. *Cha. Bathurft*, M.A. Fellow of *New College, Oxon*.
Hon. *B. Bouverie*, M.P. *Edward-ftreet, Portman-fquare*.
Rev. *James Bandinel*, D.D. Rector of *Netherbury*, near
Bridport, Dorfetfhire.
Hugh Barlow, Efq; M.P. *Lanrenny-Hall, Pembrokefh*.
Rev. *John Bull*, M.A. Curate of *Stanway, Effex*.
Rev. *Hugh Bailey*, Vicar of *Hanbury, Stafford*.
1792 Rev. *John Brown*, B.D. Vicar of *Thurfby, Cumberland*.
John Bowdler, Efq; *Hayes, Kent*.
Rev. *Jof. Banks*, LL.B. Vicar of *Hemingford Grey, Hunts*.
Rev. *Wm. Baker*, LL.B. Rector of *Lyndon, Rutland*.
Rev. *Wm. Brackenbury*, Rector of *Halton Holgate, Linc*.
Rev. *Rob. Baxter*, B.D. Fellow of *Jefus* College, *Oxford*.
Rev. *Wm. Bagfhaw*, M.A. *Buxton, Derbyfhire*.

1793 *Geo. Bridges*, Efq; *Miſtley, Eſſex.*
Major *Broke, Gower-ſtreet*
Sam. Boſanquet, Efq; *Foreſt Houſe, Layton, Eſſex.*
Rev. *W. Bree,* Vicar of *Marſton St. Lawrence, Northampt.*
Rev. *John Barton,* M. A. Vicar of *Sunning,* near *Reading.*
Rev. *Harry Barnes,* B. A. Curate of *Stoke,* near *Coventry.*
Rev. *J. F. Browning,* D. D. Rector of *Titchwell, Norfolk.*
Rev. *John Leigh Bennett, Thorpe Place,* near *Egham.*
Rev. *Cornelius Bailey,* B. D. Miniſter of *St. James's,.
Manchefter.*
Rev. *Cha.Blackſtone,* Jun. M.A. Fellow of *Winton* College;.
Mr. *William Baylis, Stapleton,* near *Briſtol.*
1794 *Thomas Browne,* Efq; *Crutched-fryers.*
Rev. *Tho. Bancroft,* M.A. Vicar of *Bolton-le-Moors, Lanc.*
Rev. *T. Breithweite,* D. D. Archdeacon of *Cheſter,*
and Rector of *Stepney.*
Rev. *Auguſtine Bulwer,* A. M. Rector of *Heydon,* with
Irmingland, Norfolk.
Rev. *J.Blenkarne,* M.A.Lecturer of *St.George in the Eaſt.*
John Blackburne, Efq; *Liverpool.*
Robert Burton, Efq; *Lincoln.*
1795 Rev. *James Burton,* D.D. Canon of *Ch. Ch. Oxon,* and
Chaplain in Ordinary to his Majeſty.
Rev. *Edw. Bradford,* B. D. Rector of *Stalbridge, Dorſet.*
Rev. *Cha. Bell,* M. A. Curate of *Iver, Buckinghamſhire.*
Rev. *Fred. Henry Barnwell, Lawſhall, Suffolk.*
Rev. *Paul Belcher,* Rector of *Heather, Leiceſterſhire.*
Rev. *Tho. Barne,* M. A. Rector of *Sotherley, Suffolk,.*
and Chaplain in Ordinary to his Majeſty.
1796 *John Brook,* Efq; of *Anſthorpe,* near *Leeds.*
William Bleamire, Efq; *Highbury Place, Iſlington.*
Rev. *Geo. Bytheſea,* M. A. Rector of *Ightham, Kent.*
Rev. *Sam. Byam,* M.A. *Univerſity* Coll. *Oxford.*
Rev. *Wm. Higgs Barker,* B.A. Chancellor of *Brecon,*
and Vicar of *Carmarthen.* Rev.

1796 Rev. *W. Boughton*, M.A. Vicar of *Blockley, Worcest.*
Rev. *Claudius Buchanan*, B.A. *Calcutta.*
Thomas Bernard, Efq; of the *Foundling Hospital.*
Rev. *Charles Ballard*, M.A. Vicar of *Chalgrove, Oxon.*
Rev. *Philip Brandon*, LL.B. Minifter of *St. George's*
Chapel, *Deal.*

1797 Rev. *Wm. Brown*, Rector of *Horton*, near *Colebrook, Bucks.*
Rev. *Thomas Barnard*, M.A. Curate of *Litcham, Norf.*
W. P. Bofville, Efq; *Ravenfield Park*, near *Doncafter.*
Rev. *Tho. Brand*, M.A. Rector of *Maulden, Bedfordfh.*
Rev. *William Barker*, B.A. *Bradford, Wiltfhire.*

1798 Rev. *John Brand*, M.A. Rector of *St. Mary at Hill*,
London.
Rev. *Thomas Briggs*, M.A. *Eton Coll. Bucks.*
Rowland Burdon, Efq; M.P. *Caftle Eden, Durham.*
John Bacon, Efq; *Newman-ftreet, Mary-le-bone.*
Thomas Bond, Efq; *Norton Houfe*, near *Dartmouth.*
William Brereton, Efq; *Upper Brook-ftreet.*
Rev. *Henry Budd*, B.A. Curate of *Aldermafton, Berks.*
Rev. *James Bollon*, M.A. Vicar of *Kelftern*, near *Louth.*
Rev. *C. F. Bond*, M.A. of *Merton, Surry.*
Rev. *Tho. Barnard*, B.D. Rector of *Steeple Langford, Wilts.*
Rev. *W. Bond*, M.A. Rector of *Steeple cum Fincham, Dorf.*

1799 *R. W. Blencowe*, Efq; of *Dallington.*
Rev. *John Briftow*, M.A. Rector of *Wefton, Notts.*
Rev. *Tho. Bargus*, M.A. Vicar of *Barkway, Herts.*
Rev. *John Healey Bromley*, M.A. Vicar of *Trinity*
Church, Kingftsn upon Hull.
Rev. *Geo. Fr. Barlow*, M.A. Rector of *Tooting, Surry.*
Edw. Berens, Efq; of *Chrift Church, Oxford.*
John Bagfhaw, Efq; of the *Oaks*, near *Sheffield.*
Rev. *John Bramfton*, M.A. Rector of *Willingdale Doe*,
and *Theydon Gamon, Effex.*

Rev,

1799 Rev. *Edw. Balme*, Vicar of *Finchingfield, Essex*.
Rev. *John Beadon*, M. A. Vicar of *Odiam, Hants*.

C.

1777 **T**HE Moft Reverend *John*, Lord Archbifhop of *Canterbury*.
1773 Right Rev. *William*, Lord Bifhop of *Chefter*.
1792 Right Rev. *Edward*, Lord Bifhop of *Carlifle*.
1790 Right Rev. *John*, Lord Bifhop of *Chichefter*.
1787 Right Hon. *Thomas*, Earl of *Clarendon*.
Right Hon. *James*, Earl of *Cardigan*.
1798 Rt. Hon. Lord Vifcount *Cremorne*.
1763 Rev. *Sam. Cooper*, D.D. Minifter of *Great Yarmouth, Norf*.
1766 Rev. *Jonathan Carter*, M. A. Rector of *Flempton with Hengrave, Suffolk*.
1767 *John Courtney*, Efq; *Beverley, Yorkfhire*.
1768 Rev. *John Charlefworth*, M. A. of *Offington, Notts*.
1769 Rev. *Thomas Clare*, D. D. *Rugby, Warwickfhire*.
Rev. *John Clowes*, M. A. Minifter of St. *John's, Manchefter*.
1771 Rev. *Potter Cole*, M. A. Vicar of *Hawkefbury, Glocefterfh*.
1772 Rev. *Thomas Cherry*, B. D. Head-Mafter of *Merchant-Taylor's* School.
Rev. *Wm. Comber*, Vicar of *Kirby Moorfide, Yorkfhire*.
Rev. *Pierrepoint Cromp*, M. A. *Frinftead, Kent*.
Jofias Cockfhut, Efq; *Ofbafton*, near *Hinckley, Leicefterfh*.
Sir *R. Chambers*, Knt. LL. D. Principal of *NewInnHallOxon*.
1773 Rev. *Thomas Cowper*, *Barton, Suffolk*.
1774 *Francis Creuzé*, Efq; *Beddington, Surry*.
John Cartier, Efq; *Bedgebury, Kent*.
1776 *Henry Courthope Campion*, Efq; *Danny, Suffex*.
Rev. *James Chelfum*, D. D. Rector of *Droxford, Hants*.
Rev. *William Colchefter*, M. A. Rector of *Holton, Suffolk*.

5   Rev.

1777 Rev. *Wm. Conybeare*, D.D. Rector of St. *Botolph, Bishopsgate*.
Rev. *Tho. Cooks*, M. A. *Abergavenny*.
1778 Rev. *William Calcott, Great Witley, Worcestershire*.
Rev. *Henry Courthope*, M. A. Vicar of *Brenchley, Kent*.
Rev. Sir *Cha. Cave*, Bart. M. A. *Thedingworth, Leicest*.
Richard Croffe, Efq; *Broomfield*, near *Bridgwater*.
1780 *George Courthope*, Junior, Efq; *Wheligh, Suffex*.
Rev. *Robert Cranmer*, M. A. Rector of *Nurfling, Hants*.
Richard Clark, Efq; Chamberlain of *London*.
Rev. *Fr. Cummings*, M.A. Vicar of *Cardington, Bedfordfh*.
1781 Mr. *John Charrington, Mile-End*.
Rev. *Jof. Chapman*, D. D. Prefident of *Trin*. Coll. *Oxon*.
1782 Rev. Sir *William Clerke*, Bart. Rector of *Bury, Lanc*.
Rev. *John Cranke*, M. A. Fellow of *Trin*. Col. *Camb*.
Rev. *John Churchill*, B. D. Rector of *Chawicy, Devon*.
1783 Rev. *J. Clapham*, M. A. Vicar of *Gigglefwick, Yorkfh*.
Rev. *H. Carter*, M. A. Rector of *Little Wittenham, Berks*.
Rev. *Hen. W. Coulthurft*, D. D. Vicar of *Hallifax, Yorkfh*.
1784 Rev. *Clement Cruttwell, Bath*.
John Cofnahan, Efq; *Douglas, Ifle of Mann*.
1785 Rev. *Roger Cockfedge*, Rector of *Whelnetham, Suffolk*.
Rev. *Tho. Cobbold*, M. A. Minifter of *St. Mary Tower, Ipfwich*.
1786 Rev. *John Clutton*, M. A. Prebendary of *Hereford*.
Rev. *John Cooper*, M. A. Rector of *Bix, Oxfordfhire*.
Rev. *Tho. Cockfhutt*, B. D. Rector of *Little Hormead, Herts*.
Mr. *Henry Creed, Afhford*, in *Kent*.
Mr. *William Complin, Enfield*.
Rev. *J. A. Carr*, M. A. Rector of *Hadfinck, Effex*.
1787 Rev. *John Cooke*, M. A. Chaplain of the Royal Hofpital, *Greenwich*.
Rev. *J. P. Cumming*, LL. B. Fellow of *New* Coll. *Oxon*.
Rev. *Henry J. Clofe*, M. A. Rector of *Hitcham*, in *Suffolk*.
Rev. *Charles Crawley*, LL. B. Rector of *Stow, Northamp*.

Rev.

1787 Rev. *George Champagne*, M.A. Rector of *Nun Eaton.*
Rev. *Tho. Chamberlayne*, M.A. Fellow of *Eton* Coll.
Thomas Chipchafe, Efq; *Durham.*

1788 *James Clitherow*, Efq; *Bofton Houfe*, near *Brentford.*
Rev. *John Cooke*, D.D. Prefident of *C.C.C. Oxon.*
Robert Corbett, Efq; *Longnor*, *Shropfhire.*
Rev. *Richard Crawley*, M.A. *Rotherfield, Suffex.*
Rev. *B. Clay*, M.A. Fellow of St. *John's* College, *Camb.*
Edw. Campion, Efq; *Chichefter.*

1789 Rev. *Tho. S. Curtis*, LL.B. Rector of *Seven Oaks, Kent.*
James Cockfhutt, Efq; *Cyfartha, Cardiff.*
Rev. *Cha. Curtis*, M.A. Rector of *St. Solihull, Warwickfh.*
Rev. *John Charter*, B.A. Vicar of *Holne, Devonfhire.*
Rev. *Morgan Cove*, LL.B. Rector of *Eton Bifhop, Heref.*
Rev. *Thomas Crick*, M.A. Rector of *Little Thurlow*,
    and Vicar of *Mildenhall, Suffolk.*
Samuel Crawley, Efq; *Ragnall-Hall, Nottinghamfh.*
Rev. *W. Cookfon*, M.A. *Forncet, Long-Stretton, Norf.*
Rev. *Roger Clough*, Rector of *Thakeham, Suffex.*

1790 Rev. *W. Crawford*, M.A. Archdeacon of *Carmarthen.*
Rev. *Jofeph Cartwright, Dudley, Worcefterfhire.*
Rev. *Ar. R. Chauvel*, M.A. Rector of *Stanmore, Midd.*
Rev. *Alex. Cromleholme*, M.A. Rector of *Sherrington*,
    near *Newport Pagnel.*
Tho. Cave, Efq; *Tokenhoufe-yard.*
Rev. *John Carver*, M.A. Rector of *Whifton, Yorkfhire.*
Rev. *Henry Chatfield*, Rector of *Balcomb, Suffex.*
Rev. *James Cowe*, M.A. Vicar of *Sunbury, Middlefex.*

1791 *William Conftable*, Efq; *Burwafh*, in *Suffex.*
Rev. *Geo. Owen Cambridge*, M.A. Prebendary of *Ely*
Rev. *George Cope*, M.A. Prebendary of *Hereford.*

1792 Rev. *Wm. Carpenter*, D.D. Prebendary of *Exeter*, and
    Rector of *Hafelbeare Briant, Dorfetfhire.*

4   *Wm.*

1792 *Wm. Cooper*, Eſq; *Caton, Lancaſhire.*
1793 Rev. *Tho. Carlyon*, M. A. Fellow of *Pembroke Hall, Camb.*
Wm. Craze, Eſq; *Hornſey, Middleſex.*
John Berridge Cholwich, Eſq; *Farringdon Houſe, Devonſh.*
Mr. *William Cardale, Bedford-row, London.*
1794 Rev. *Charles Cowley*, M. A. Rector of *Goldhanger, Eſſex.*
Rev. *S. Crowther*, M. A. Fellow of *New* College, *Oxon.*
Rev. *Benj. Charlewood*, B. A. *Oak Hill, Cheadle, Staffordſh.*
Rev. *William Cole*, D. D. Prebendary of *Weſtminſter.*
Mr. *John Chippindale, Bunhill-row, Moorfields.*
Mr. *John Caſs, High-ſtreet, Whitechapel.*
Mr. *Clutton, Cuckfield.*
Rev. *Ralph Churton*, M. A. Rector of *Middleton Cheney,* near *Banbury.*
Rev. *John Crofts*, M. A. Aſſiſtant Miniſter at *Portland Chapel.*
1795 Rev. *Edw. Conyers*, M. A. Vicar of *Epping, Eſſex.*
William Curteis, Eſq; *Friday-ſtreet.*
Rev. *Thomas Cogan*, M. A. Vicar of *Eaſtdeane, Suſſex.*
Rev. *Wm. Cornwallis*, M. A. Rector of *Witterſham, Kent.*
Rev. *R. Chaplin*, LL. B. Rector of *Averſham cum Kelham, Newark.*
1796 *Richard Cox*, Eſq; *Craig's-court.*
Richard Creyke, Eſq; Governor of the Royal Hoſpital at *Plymouth.*
1797 Rev. *Richard Coleman, Dymchurch, Kent.*
Rev. *Thomas Craſter*, M. A. Prebendary of *Lincoln.*
Rev. *John Cleaver*, D. D. Rector of *Slingſby, Yorkſh.*
Rev. *Thomas Coney*, Rector of *Batcombe, Somerſet.*
Rev. *Henry Collet*, M. A. *Tewkeſbury, Gloceſterſhire.*
Rev. *W. Craven*, D. D. Maſter of St. *John's* Coll. *Camb.*
John George Clarke, Eſq; *King's Bench Walk, Temple.*
Thomas Clarke, Eſq; *Swakeley Houſe*, near *Uxbridge.*
Rev. *Septimus Collinſon*, D. D. Provoſt of *Queen's* College, *Oxford.*

F   Rev.

1797 *Richard Clarke*, Efq; *Harcourt Buildings, Temple.*
1798 Mr. *James Coope, Northern, Chefhire.*
Rev. *James Camplin*, M. A. Rector of *Clutworthy, Somerf.*
Rev. *Robert Croft*, M. A. Canon Refidentiary of *York.*
Thomas Cadell, Efq; Alderman of *London.*
Rev. *Colfon Carr,* LL.B. Vicar of *Ealing, Middlefex.*
Mr. *Anthony Clerke, Caroline-Place, Foundling Hofpital.*
Rev. *Francis Capper,* M. A. Rector of *Earlfoham, Suffolk.*
Rev. *Charles Cooper,* D. D. Prebendary of *Durham.*
Rev. *John Cooke,* M. A. Head Mafter of the Royal
Free Grammar School, *Birmingham.*
Rev. *Henry Campbell,* B. A. of *Chrift Church Oxford.*
Rev. *G. T. Carwithen,* Curate of *Newton St. Agnes, Devon.*
Rev. *Abr. John Crefpin,* Vicar of *Renhold, Bedfordfhire.*
Geo. Cherry, Efq; Commiffioner of the Victualling Board.
1799 Rev. *Richard Carveth,* B. A. of *Elmore, Gloceflerfhire.*
Rev. *Samuel Cole,* Rector of *Brettenham, Suffolk.*
Bicknell Coney, Efq; *Enfield, Middlefex.*
Rev. *Clement Cottrell, Hadleigh, Herts.*
Rev. *Edw. Cooper,* Rector of *Hamflall Ridware, Stafford.*
John Cook, Efq; *Tunford,* near *Chefhunt, Herts.*
Rev. *R. J. Carr,* M. A. Rector of *Limpifham, Somerfet.*

D.

1769 HON. and Rt. Rev. *Shute,* Lord Bifhop of *Durham.*
1796 Hon. and Right Rev. *William,* Lord Bifhop of
St. *David's.*
1756 Right Honourable *William,* Earl of *Dartmouth.*
1795 Right Honourable *John,* Earl of *Darnley.*
1746 Mr. *Peter Dobrée* of *Guernfey.*
1761 Rev. *Lewis de la Chaumette,* Minifter of the *French*
London Church.
1763 Rev. *Daniel Dumaresq,* D. D. Prebendary of *Salifbury.*
1764 Rev. *Samuel Denne,* M. A. Vicar of *Wilmington, Kent.*
—— *Dilling-*

1770 —— *Dillingham*, Efq; *Grundifburg*, *near Ipfwich*, *Suffolk*.
1773 Rev. *William Difney*, D. D. Rector of *Pluckley*, *Kent*.
1776 Rev. *William Dodwell*, M. A. Rector of *Welby*, *Lincolnfhire*.
1777 Rev. *Henry-Jerome De Salis*, D.D. Rector of St. *Antho-
    lin's*, *London*, and Chaplain in Ordinary to His Majefty.
    Rev. *William Dyer*, M.A. Rector of *Leaden Roding*, *Effex*.
1778 Rev. *Andrew Downes*, M. A. Vicar of *Witham*, *Effex*.
    John Dorville, Efq; *Raven's Court*, *Hammerfmith*.
    Rev. *Heneage Dering*, D. D. Prebendary of *Canterbury*.
1779 *John-Englifh Dolben*, Efq; *Finedon*, *Northamptonfhire*.
1781 Rev. *John Drake*, LL.D. Rector of *Amerfham*, *Bucks*.
    Rev. *B. Downing*, LL.B. Rector of *Quainton*, *Aylefbury*.
1782 Mr. *Thomas Dornford*, *Philpot-lane*, *London*.
1783 Rev. *Noel Digby*, M.A. Rector of *Brixton*, *Ifle of Wight*.
1784 Rev. *J. Daubeney*, M.A. Rector of *Stratton*, *Cirencefter*.
    Rev. *John Douglas*, D. D. Vicar of *Beenham*, *Berks*.
1785 Rev. *Henry H. Darby*, M.A. of *Groton*, *Suffolk*.
1786 Rev. *George-William-Auriol-Hay Drummond*, M. A.
    Prebendary of *York*, and Vicar of *Brodfworth*, *Yorkfh*.
    Rev. *Philip Douglas*, D. D. Mafter of *C. C. C. Camb*.
    Rev. *Thomas Dampier*, D. D. Dean of *Rochefter*.
1787 Rev. *Thomas Drake*, D. D. Vicar of *Rochdale*, *Lanc*.
    Rev. *Henry Drummond*, Rector of *Fawley*, *Hants*.
    Rev. *Arthur Dodwell*, of the *Clofe*, *Salifbury*.
    Rev. *John Dampier*, M. A. Rector of *Weftmeon*, *Hants*.
    Rev. *J. L. Dayrell*, Rector of *Lillingfton Dayrell*, *Bucks*.
    Rev. *George Downing*, M.A. Prebendary of *Ely*.
    Rev. *J. Darwin*, M. A. Rector of *Carlton Scroop*, *Linc*.
1788 Rev. *Ed. A. H. Drummond*, D.D. Rector of *Hadleigh*,
    Suffolk.
1789 Rev. *Tho. Dethick*, M. A. *Bridgnorth*, *Shropfhire*.
1790 Rev. *Wm. Dowfon*, D. D. Principal of *St. Edmund's-
    Hall*, *Oxford*.

1790 Rev. *Jonathan Davies*, D.D. Provoſt of *Eton* College.
Tho. Dudley, Eſq; *Shut-End*, near *Stourbridge*.
George Downing, Eſq; *Lincoln's-Inn*.
Rev. *John Dudley*, Rector of *Himley*, near *Stourbridge*.
Lieut. Col. *Dury*, *Hadley*, *Midaleſex*.
Rev. *John Duppa*, M. A. *Batchley*, *Herefordſhire*.
1791 Rev. *Rob. Douglas*, LL.B. Rector of *Salwarp*, near *Worceſt*.
John Dilnot, Eſq; *Sandwich*, *Kent*.
William Danby, Eſq; *Swinton*, *Yorkſhire*.
Wm. Lloyd Doulben, Eſq; *Rhiwacdog*, *Merionethſh*.
Rev. *Ric. Davies*, M. A. Uſher of *Bangor* School.
1792 *Wriotheſly Digby*, Eſq; *Meriden*, *Warwick*.
1793 *Edward Dixon*, Eſq; *Dudley*, *Worceſterſhire*.
Rev. *Samuel Dent*, Rector of St. *George's*, in *Grenada*.
1794 Rev. *Hen. Dearman*, B. A. Rector of *Ickenham*, *Middleſex*.
Rev. *Hugh Davies*, Rector of *Aber*, near *Bangor*.
Rev. *James Deare*, Vicar of *Bures St. Mary*, *Suffolk*.
1795 Mr. *Robert Deane*, of *Holy Croſs*, *Weſtgate*, *Canterbury*.
Rev. *Tho. W. Dalby*, M. A. Vicar of *Chippenham*, *Wilts*.
Mr. *Wm. Davis*, of *Londwater*, near *Beaconsfield*.
Rev. *Cha. Daubeney*, LL.B. Fellow of *Winton College*.
Rev. *H. M. Davies*, M.A. Vicar of *Weſtwell*, *Kent*.
1796 Rev. *P. Dickinſon*, M. A. Vicar of *Biſhop's Stortford*.
1797 Rev. *Edward Dickenſon*, B. D. Rector of *Stafford*.
Rev. *James Dowland*, LL.B. Rector of *Clenſtone*, *Dorſet*.
Rev. *Richard Darke*, M.A. Rector of *Grafton Flyford*,
Worceſterſhire.
John Dixon, Eſq; *Walbrook*.
Rev. *John Dewe*, M.A. Rector of *Brendſal*, *Derbyſhire*.
John Smith Daintrey, Eſq; *Macclesfield*, *Cheſhire*.
Rev. *Reynold Davies*, B.A. Curate of *Streatham*, *Surry*.
Jeremiah Dyſon, Eſq; *Brompton Park Houſe*.
1798 *Robert Drummond*, Eſq; *Charing Croſs*, *London*.
A. B. Drummond, Eſq; *Ditto*.

John

1798 *John Drummond*, Eſq; *Ditto.*
Charles Drummond, Eſq; *Ditto.*
Rev. *P. S. Dodd*, B. A. *Camberwell, Surry.*
Rev. *William Dickens*, M. A. *Cherwelton*, near *Daventry.*
John Dodſworth, Eſq; of *York.*
1799 Rev. *Tho. Dennis*, S. C. L. Curate of *Willand, Devon.*
Rev. *Wm. Davies*, M. A. Vicar of *Wooton Baſſet, Wilts.*
Rev. *Edw. Dawkins*, M. A. Rector of *Weſt Dean, Wilts.*

E

1775 **H**ON. and Right Rev. *James*, Lord Biſhop of *Ely.*
1776   Right Rev. *Henry Reginald*, Lord Biſhop of *Exeter.*
1777 Right Rev. *John*, Lord Biſhop of *Elphin.*
1792 Right Hon. Lord *Eardley.*
1764 Rev. *Edward Edwards*, M. A. Archdeacon of *Brecon.*
1767 Rev. *Stephen Eaton*, M. A. Archdeacon of *Middleſex.*
1773 Rev. *Thomas Evans*, D. D. Archdeacon of *Worceſter.*
1776 Rev. *John Emeris*, M. A. Rector of *Tetford*, near *Louth.*
Iſaac Ecles, Eſq; *Alboure, Suſſex.*
1777 Rev. *Allan H. Eccles*, M. A. Rector of *Bow, Middleſex.*
1781 Rev. *Joſeph Eyre*, M. A. Vicar of St. *Giles', Reading.*
Rev. *John Eveleigh*, D. D. Provoſt of *Oriel* Coll. *Oxon.*
Rev. *James Edwards*, B. D. Vicar of *Fairford, Gloceſterſh.*
1782 Rev. *James Evans*, M. A. Rector of St. *Olave's, Southwark.*
1783 *Gregory Elſley*, Eſq; of *Patrick-Brompton*, near *Bedal.*
1785 Rev. *Bartholomew Edwards*, Rector of *Hetherſet, Norfolk.*
1786 Rev. *P. Elers*, M. A. Rector of *Riſhangles, Suffolk.*
1787 Rev. *John Ekins*, D. D. Dean of *Saliſbury.*
John E. W. Emerton, Eſq; *Thrumpton, Notts.*
1788 Rev. *George Ediſon*, M. A. Rector of *Stock*, in *Eſſex.*
Rev. *Edw. Edwards*, M. A. Lecturer of *Lynn Regis, Norf.*
Rev. *Geo. Evans*, M. A. Rector of *Humber*, near *Leominſter.*
Rev. *Edward Edwards*, *Huntingdon.*

Rev.

1789 Rev. *O. P. Edwardes*, M. A. Rector of *St. Barthol.* the
Great, *London*.

Mr. *Francis Eginton*, *Handſworth*, near *Birmingham*.

1791 Rev. *H. W. Eyton*, *Leeſwood-Hall*, *Flintſhire*.

1792 Rev. *W. Eaſton*, B.D. Vicar of *Barrow*, near *Loughborough*.

1793 Rev. *T. Evanſin*, M. A. Rector of *Gr. Catworth*, *Hunts*.

Mr. *Edward Jacob Eve*, *Linton*, *Cambridgeſhire*.

1794 Rev. *H. Holland Edwards*, M. A. Rector of *Waddeſdon*.

1795 Mr. *J ſeph Earle*, *Watling-ſtreet*.

Rev. *Edw. Eſtcourt*, D. D. of *Newnton*, *Wilts*.

1796 Rev. *C. L. Edridge*, M. A. Vicar of *Eaſt* and *Weſt Rud-
ham*, *Norfolk*, and Chaplain in Ordinary to his Majeſty.

Rev. *J. Ellis*, M.A. of *Kyffdu*, near *Llanwrſt*, *Denbighſh*.

Rev. *G. Edmonſtone*, M. A. Vicar of *Addington*, *Surry*.

Rev. *Edw. Embry*, Curate of St. *Paul's*, *Covent-Garden*.

Rev. *James Etty*, M. A. Rector of *Whitchurch*, *Oxon*.

1797 Rev. *Daniel Everard*, M. A. Rector of *Stanhoe*, *Norfolk*.

John Evered, Eſq; *Hi'l* Houſe, near *Bridgwater*.

Rev. *William England*, *Stafford*, near *Dorcheſter*, *Dorſe'ſh*.

Rev. *Ja. Evans*, M. A. Rector of *South Reſton*, *Linc*.

1798 *George Edwards*, Eſq; *Henlon*, *Bedfordſhire*.

Rev. *John Eyre*, Canon Reſidentiary of *York*.

1799 Rev. *John Elliſon*, Curate of *Newcaſtle* upon *Tyne*

F.

1757 REV. *Thomas Fownes*, M. A. Vicar of *Brixham*, *Devon*.
Rev. *Rob. P. Finch*, D.D. Prebendary of *Weſtminſter*.

1761 *Tho. Edwards Freeman*, Eſq;

1771 Rev. *John Fox*, M. A. *Etton*, *Yorkſhire*.

1776 Rev. *John Fountayne*, D. D. Dean of *York*.

1777 *James Fenoulhet*, Eſq; *Dean-ſtreet*, *Soho*.

Rev. *Henry Fly*, D. D. Rector of St. *Auguſtin's*, *London*.

1778 Rev. *J. Fallowfield*, M. A. Fellow of *Clare Hall*, *Camb*.

Rev.

1778 Rev. *R. Fountaine*, M.A. Vicar of *Sutton at Hone, Kent*.
1779 Rev. *Wm. Flamank*, D.D. Rector of *Glympton, Oxon*.
Rev. *John Foley*, M.A.Rector of *Chriſt-church, Middleſex*
1780 Rev. *Ric. Farrer*, Rector of *Aſhley, Northamptonſhire*.
1782 Rev. *Edm. Ferrers*, M.A. Rector of *Cheriton, Hants*.
1783 Rev.*Rob.Foote*, M.A. Rector of *Boughton Malherb, Kent*.
John Foote, Eſq; *Charlton-Place, Kent*.
Sir *Beverſham Filmer*, Bart. *King's Road, Bedford-Row*.
1785 Rev. *Thomas Fowle*, Vicar of *Kentbury, Berks*.
1786 Rev. Sir *John Fagg*, Bart. M.A. of *Myſtole* in *Kent*.
Rev. *William Foſter*, D.D Fellow of *Eton* College.
Rev. *Richard Frank*, D.D. Rector of *Alderton, Suffolk*.
1787 Rev. *Edward Foyle*, M.A. Rector of *Kimpton, Hants*.
John Fothergill, Eſq; *Micklegate, York*.
Mr. *William Fiſher, Lancaſter*.
Matthew Fletcher, Eſq; *Clifton* near *Mancheſter*.
Edward James Foote, Eſq; Captain of the Royal Navy.
1788 Rev. *Hen. Ford*, LL.D. Principal of *Magd. Hall, Oxon*.
John Freeman, Eſq; *Lotton, Herefordſhire*.
1789 *Thomas Finch*, Eſq; *Great Ormond-ſtreet*.
Oliver Farrer, Eſq; *Bedford-Square*.
1790 Rev. *Cha. Fynes*, LL.D. Prebendary of *Weſtminſter*.
Rev. *Thomas Ferris*, D.D. Dean of *Battle*, in *Suſſex*.
Rev.*Rob.Fowler*,LL.B. Rector of*Warboys, Huntingdonſh*.
1791 *John Fane*, Eſq; *Wormſley, Oxfordſhire*.
1792 Rev.*Branſby Francis*, M.A. Rector of *Edgefield, Norfolk*.
Rev.*Wm. Finch*, Miniſter of St. *Helen*, near *Preſcot*.
Nich. Lacey Fry, Eſq; *Streatham, Surry*.
John Franklin, Eſq; *Llanmihangle, Glamorgan*.
1793 *Henry Feilden*, Eſq; *Blackburne, Lancaſhire*.
1794 Rev. *Charles Favell*, M.A. Rector of *Brington, Hunts*.
Rev. *John Farrer*, Vicar of *Stanwix, Cumberland*.
1796 Rev.*Hugh Fraſer*,M.A. Rector of St.*Martin's, Ludgate*.
Rev. *Geo. Feachem*, M.A. Curate of *Dorking, Surry*.

6 Rev.

1796 Rev. *Wm. Floyer,* Vicar of *Stinsford, Dorſetſhire.*
Rev. *Tho. Farmer,* M.A. Rector of St. *Luke's, Old-ſtreet.*
Rev. *J. Folds,* Lecturer of *Bolton-le-Moors, Lancaſhire.*
Rev. *John Fiſher,* D.D. Canon of *Windſor,* and Clerk
of the Cloſet to his Majeſty.
Rev. *Daniel Finch,* B.D. Prebendary of *Glouceſter.*
1798 Rev. *I. T. Fleſher,* M.A. Rector of *Tiffield, Northamptonſh.*
Devy Fearon, M.D. *Ely Place, London.*
Mr. *John Fennel,* of the *Cuſtom Houſe.*
Rev. *G. Stanley Faber,* M.A. Fellow of *Lincoln* Coll. *Oxf.*
Rev. *W. J. French,* M.A. Rector of *Vange, Eſſex.*
1799 Rev. *James Franks,* M.A. Curate of *Halifax, Yorkſhire.*

G.

1776 **R**IGHT Rev. *Richard,* Lord Biſhop of *Gloceſter.*
1786 Right Honourable Lord Viſcount *Galway.*
1754 Rev. *John Gooch,* D.D. Prebendary of *Ely.*
1757 Rev. *Samuel Glaſſe,* D.D. Rector of *Wanſtead,* and
Chaplain in Ordinary to His Majeſty.
1768 *Edward Green,* Eſq; *Lawford-hall,* near *Dedham.*
Rev. *John Ruſſell Greenhill,* LL.D. Rector of *Fring-*
ford, Oxfordſhire, and of *Marſh Gibbon, Bucks.*
1771 Rev. *John Gandy,* M.A. Vicar of St. *Andrew's, Plymouth.*
1773 Rev. *Philip Griffin,* LL.D. Rector of *Warnford, Hants.*
Rev. *William Gee,* Rector of St. *Stephen's, Ipſwich.*
1774 *Francis Goſling,* Eſq; Banker, in *Fleet-ſtreet.*
1776 Rev. *E. Garden,* Reader to the Hon. Society of *Gray's-Inn.*
Rev. *Thomas Lechmere Grimwood,* D.D. Rector of
Bramſton, Norfolk, and Lecturer of *Dedham, Eſſex.*
1777 Rev. *John Gooch,* M.A. Archdeacon of *Sudbury.*
Rev. *Geo. Gaſkin,* D.D. Rector of St. *Bene't Grace-church.*
1778 Hon. and Rev. *Charles Graham,* of *Hertingfordbury.*
1781 Rev. *John Garret,* B.A. Maſter of the Grammar-School
of *Chudleigh, Devonſhire.*

4   Rev.

1783 Rev. *R. B. Gabriel*, D.D. Rector of *Harlington, Middleſex.*
1784 *Thomas Goulton*, Eſq; near *Brigg, Lincolnſhire.*
1786 Rev. *Walthall Gretton, Audlem,* near *Namptwich.*
 Rev. *Geo. H. Glaſſe,* M.A. Rector of *Hanwell, Middleſex.*
 Rev. *Hen. Good,* D.D. Miniſter of *Wimborn Minſter, Dorſ.*
 John Matthew Grimwood, Eſq; *Hatton-Garden.*
 Rev. *Thomas Giſborne,* M.A. *Yoxall Lodge, Staffordſh.*
1787 Rev. *Rob. Gwilt,* M.A. Rector of *Icklingham, Suffolk.*
 Henry Grimſton, Eſq; *Weſlow, Yorkſhire.*
 Rev. *Browne Griſdale,* D.D. Rector of *Bowneſs, Cumb.*
 Rev. *Val. Grantham,* M.A. Rector of *Odel, Bedfordſh.*
 Sir *I. W. S. Gardiner,* Bart. *Clerk Hill, Lancaſhire.*
 Rev. *Richard Grylls,* LL. B. of *Helſtone, Cornwall.*
 Rev. *James Graves,* Miniſter of St. *John's, Beverley.*
 John Goodeve, Eſq; *Kennington-lane, Lambeth.*
1788 Rev. *Peter Gunning,* D. D. Rector of *Deynton,* and of
  Farmborough, near *Bath.*
 Joſeph Gape, Eſq; *Bridge-ſtreet, Weſtminſter.*
 Hon. *Booth Grey,* of *Wincham, Cheſhire.*
 Rev. *John Gilby,* LL. B. Rector of *Barmſton, Bridlington.*
 Rev. *Ric. Griffith,* Rector of *Llandegven, Angleſey.*
 Rev. *Rob. Gray,* M. A. Rector of *Creyke, Yorkſhire.*
1789 Rev. *Edm. Gilbert,* Rector of *Helland, Cornwall.*
 Rev. *Edw. Goodwin,* Miniſter of *Attercliffe, Sheffield.*
 Thomas Green, Eſq; *Harborn,* near *Birmingham.*
 Mr. *John Gibbons, Birmingham.*
 Mr. *Joſeph Gibbs, Birmingham.*
 Golding Griggs, Eſq; *Meſſing,* in *Eſſex.*
 Rev. *Joſeph Gregory,* St. *Martin's, Leiceſter.*
1790 Rev. *John Grindlay,* L.L. D. *Kennington, Surry.*
 John Groves, Eſq; *Sloane-ſtreet, Chelſea.*
 Rev. *Moſes Grant,* Rector of *Nalton, Haverford Weſt.*
 Charles Grant, Eſq; *Clapham.*

      G   Rev.

1790 Rev. *Sam. Goodenough,* LL.D. Canon of *Windfor.*
1791 Rev. *John Gibbons,* M. A. Vicar of *Piddletown, Dorfet.*
    Charles Greenwood, Efq; *Craig's-court, Charing Crofs.*
    William Gofling, Efq; Banker, in *Fleet-ftreet.*
    Hen. Green, Efq; M. A. *Roleftone Hall, Leiceft.*
    Rev. *Hugh Griffith,* M. A. *Edorn, Carnarvonfhire.*
    Rev. *E. Gibert,* Preacher at the *French* Chapel, St. *James's.*
    Rev *John Glover,* B. A. Curate of *Brabrooke, Northamp.*
    Jofeph Grote, Efq; *Upper Grofvenor Street, London.*
    Rev. *John Green,* B. D. Fellow of *Sidney* Coll. *Camb.*
    John Gifborne, Efq; *Holly Bufh Hall,* near *Tutbury, Staff.*
1792 Rev. *Edw. Glover,* M. A. Vicar of *Barmer, Norfolk.*
    Rev. *Wm. Green,* M. A. Vice Prin. of *Magd. Hall, Oxf.*
    William Gilby, M. D. of *Birmingham.*
1793 Rev. *Benjamin Grifdale, Withington, Glocefterfhire.*
    Rev. *Henry Good,.* M. A. Rector of *Stockton, Wilts.*
    Rev. *Theo. Girdleftone,* Rector of *Beaconfthorpe, Norfolk.*
    Rev. *Ch. Grape,* D. D. Rect. of *Horftead* and *Coltifhall, Norf.*
1794 Rev. *Cha. de Guiffardiere,* M. A. Rect. of *Newington, Surry.*
    Rev. *Nicholas Gay,* Vicat of *Upper Ottery, Devon.*
    Rev. *Peter Geary,* M. A. Fellow of *Trinity* Coll. *Oxon.*
    H. Gardiner, Efq; *Wandfworth, Surry.*
    Rev. *Wm. Gray,* M. A.
    Edw. Grove, Efq; City of *Litchfield.*
1795 Rev. *Jofeph Gunning,* M. A. Vicar of *Sutton, Suffolk.*
    Rev. *John Gray,* Vicar of *Hilbaldftowe,* near *Brigg, Linc.*
    Will. Goffip, Efq; *Hatfield,* near *Doncafter.*
    Mr. *John Greaves, Bakewell, Derbyfhire.*
    Rev. *Tho. Green,* D. D. Rector of *Bramber, Suffex.*
    Rev. *Fergus Grabam,* LL.D. Rector of *Arthuret, Cumberl.*
1796 Rev. *Grif. Griffith,* B. A. Rector of St. *Paul's, Shadwell.*
    Richard Gray, Efq; *Ealing, Middlefex.*

Rev.

1796 Rev. *H. Davies Griffith*, M.A. *Caerbun, Carnarvonfh.*
      Rev. Sir *Adam Gordon*, Bart. Prebendary of *Briftol.*
1797 Rev. *Geo. Gibfon,* Mafter of *Carlifle* Houfe Academy, *Surry.*
      Andrew Guy, Efq; *Barford,* near *Bridgwater.*
      Mr. *Thomas Greenalgh,* St. *Helen's, Lancafhire.*
1798 Rev. *James Griffith,* M.A. Fellow of Univ. Coll. *Oxon.*
      Rev. *T. F. Gower,* B.A. *Witham, Effex.*
      Mr. *John Griffin, Stewart Street, Spitalfields.*
      Rev. —— *Griffith,* Mafter of *Warminfter* School, *Wilts.*
      Rev.*Cha.Green,*M.A.Rectorof *Hemingford Abbot's,Hunts.*
      Rev. *John Garnett,* M.A. Prebendary of *Winton,* and
      Chaplain in Ordinary to his Majefty.
      Rev. *Peter Guillebaud,* B.A. Curate of St. *Auguftin's,
      London.*

H.

1750 **R**IGHT Rev. *John,* Lord Bifhop of *Hereford.*
1749   Rev. *Ric. Humfrey,* M. A. Rector of *Thorpe, Norf.*
1761 Rev.*E.Hughes,* M.A.Rectorof *Shenington,* near *Banbury.*
1764 Rev. *Edm. Harvey,* Rector of *Finningley, Nottinghamfh.*
1765 Right Hon. *Thomas Harley,* M.P. Alderman of *London.*
1767 Rev. *Anthony Hamilton,* D.D. Archdeacon of *Colchefter.*
1769 Rev. *Peter Haddon,* M.A. Vicar of *Leeds, Yorkfhire.*
1770 Rev. *John Hutchings,* Rector of *Dittifham, Devon.*
1772 Rev. *Daniel Hill,* M. A. Vicar of *Eaftmalling, Kent.*
1773 *Thomas Bayley Hall,* Efq; *Hermitage, Chefhire.*
      Rev. *Reginald Heber,* M. A. Rector of *Malpas, Chefhire.*
1775 *Thomas Holbeche,* Efq; *Hill Court, Worcefterfhire.*
1777 *John Heywood,* Efq; *Paper-Buildings, Temple.*
      Rev. *Geo. Holiwell,* B. D. Rector of *Irby,* near *Caiftor,*
      Rev. *R. Hamilton,* LL.D. Vicar of St. *Olave, Jewry.*
      Rev. *William Huffey,* M. A; Rector of *Sandhurft, Kent.*

1777 *Thomas Hammerſley*, Eſq; Banker, *Pall-Mall*.
1778 Rev. *Geo. W. Hand*, M. A. Archdeacon of *Dorſet*.
1779 Rev. *Thomas Heberden*, M. A. Canon of *Exeter*.
      Rev. *James Hare*, M.A. Rector of *Colne St. Dennis, Wilts*.
      Rev. *Benj. Hall*, B. D. Senior Vicar-Choral of *Llandaff*.
1780 Rev. *John Heathfield, Northaw, Hertfordſhire*.
1781 *Samuel Hawkins*, Eſq; *Goodman's-fields*.
      Rev. *Ric. Harington*, M.A. Rector of *Hagley, Worceſterſh*.
1782 Rev. *Geoffrey Hornby*, Rector of *Winwick, Lancaſh*.
      Rev. *Henry Hutton*, B. D. Rector of *Beaumont, Eſſex*.
      Rev. *Benjamin Heath*, D. D. Fellow of *Eton* College.
      Rev. *Geo. Hearne*, Rector of *St. Alphage, Canterbury*.
1783 Rev. *Herbert Hill*, M. A. Chaplain to the *Engliſh*
      Factory at *Liſbon*.
      Rev. *John Hutton*, B. D. Vicar of *Burton*, in *Kendal*.
1784 *Tho. H. Hodges*, Eſq; *Hempſtead Place*, near *Cranbrooke*.
      Rev. *Edward Hawtrey*, M.A. Rector of *Monxton, Hants*.
1785 Rev. *James Hodgſon*, M. A. Rector of *Keſton, Kent*.
      Rev. *George Hayward*, Vicar of *Froceſter, Gloceſterſhire*.
      Rev.*William Hunter*, M.A. Rector of *St. Ann, Middleſex*.
1786 Rev. *Wm. Herringham*, B.D. Rector of *Chadwell, Eſſex*.
1787 Rev. *Wilfred Huddleſtone*, M. A. Miniſter of *St. Nicho-*
      las, Whitehaven.
      Rev. *Manning Holden*, LL.B. Rector of *Weeting, Norfolk*.
      Rev. *Henry Heathcote*, M. A. Rector of *Walton, Lanc*.
      Rev. *Joſ. Hepworth*, M. A. *North Walſham, Norf*.
      John Sidney Hawkins, Eſq; *Guildford-ſtreet*.
      Rev. *Robert Hawker*, D. D. Vicar of *Charles, Plymouth*.
      Rev. *William Hawkins*, M.A. *Bampton, Oxfordſhire*.
      Rev. *George Harper*, M. A. Fellow of *Brazen Noſe* Coll.
      Oxon, and one of His Majeſty's Preachers at *Whitehall*.
      Rev. *John Hey*, D.D. Rector of *Paſſenham, Stony-Stratf*.
      Rev. *David Hughes*, D.D. Fellow of *Jeſus* Coll. *Oxon*.

Mr.

1787 Mr. *William Hardman, Manchester.*
Mr. *John Harrop, Saddleworth,* near *Manchester.*
Rev. *J. Hildyard,* B. A. *Monk's Eleigh, Suffolk.*
Rev. *Ric. Hart,* M. A. Vicar of St. *George's, Glouc.*
Rev. *Sam. Hey,* M. A. Vicar of *Steeple Ashton, Wilts.*
1788 *Henry Hugh Hoare,* Esq; Banker, in *Fleet-street.*
Thomas B. Howell, Esq;
Rev. *John Hinton,* Rector of *Chawton, Hants.*
John Hole, Esq; *Islington.*
Rev. *Thomas Horne,* D. D. Master of *Chiswick* School.
Rev. *John Howes,* Vicar of *Fordingbridge, Hants.*
1789 Mr. *Wm. Holden, Birmingham.*
Thomas Hall, Esq; *Preston Candover, Hampshire.*
Henry Hoare, Esq; Banker, in *Fleet-street.*
Rev. *James Hadow,* M. A. Vicar of *Sundon, Bedfordsh.*
Rev. *Wm. Hughes,* Curate of *Albury, Herts.*
Rev. *J. Hayes,* M.A. Rector of *Everdon, Northamptonsh.*
William Hey, Esq; F. R. S. Surgeon, in *Leeds.*
1790 Rev. *Rob. Holt,* M.A. Rector of *Finmere,* near *Buckingham.*
Thomas Heming, Esq; *Hillingdon, Middlesex.*
Benj. Harrison, Esq; Treasurer of *Guy's-Hospital.*
Rev. *R. F. Howman,* B. A. Rector of *Hockering, Norf.*
Rev. *Wm. Hawtayne,* Rector of *Elstree, Herts.*
Rev. *Tho. Holme, Upholland,* near *Wigan.*
Rev. *T. R. Hooker,* M. A. Rector of *Rottindean, Sussex.*
Mr. *James Horwood, Newgate-market.*
Isaac Hobhouse, Esq; *Westbury upon Trym,* near *Bristol.*
George Hardinge, Esq; M. P. *Lincoln's-Inn.*
Rev. *Tho. Hughes,* M. A. Prebendary of *Westminster.*
Thomas Hobhouse, Esq; of the *Inner-Temple.*
Rev. *John Hallam,* D. D. Dean of *Bristol.*
Mr. *Brook A. Hurlock, Dedham, Essex.*
Rev. *Henry Hunter,* Rector of *Thurnscoe, Yorkshire.*
Rev. *Wm. Hedges,* M. A. Rector of *Thriberg, Yorkshire.*

Rev.

1790 Rev. *John Harvey*, LL. B. *Wilburton*, in the Iſle of *Ely*.
Sir *Edm. C. Hartopp*, Bart. *Four Oaks, Sutton Coldfield*.
Rev. *James Long Hutton*, M. A. *Buckingham*.
Rev. *Hugh Hornby*, Rector of St. *Michael's, Lancaſhire*.
1791 Rev. *T. Hen. Hume*, M. A. Vicar of *Broad Hinton, Wilts*.
Rev. *Geo. If. Huntingford*, D.D. Warden of *Winton* Coll.
Rev. *J. Hewlett*, B.D. Lecturer of St. *Vedaſt's, Foſter-lane*.
Richard *Cope Hopton*, Eſq; *Canon-Frome, Herefordſhire*.
Rev. *Ric. Harvey*, M. A. Vicar of *Eaſtry, Kent*.
Rev. *Cha. Hayward*, B. A. Curate of *Copford, Eſſex*.
Rev. *Geo. Avery Hatch*, M. A. Rector of St. *Matthew,
    Friday-ſtreet*.
1792 Rev. *Hen. Hodgkinſon*, M. A. Chaplain to the County
    Jail, *Reading*.
Rev. *John Hughes*, B.A. Vicar of *Eglwys Fach, Denbighſh*.
Rev. *John Hawkins*, Vicar of *Halſted, Eſſex*.
Rev. *Rob. M. Humphreys*, M. A. *Rhyd Lanfair*, near
    Llanwrſt, Denbyſhire.
Rev. *Sam. Heyrick*, M.A. Rector of *Brampton, Northamp*.
1793 *William Hazlewood*, Gent. *Bridgnorth, Shropſhire*.
Rev. *Ric. Huſband*, M. A. Vicar of *Weſtmalling, Kent*.
Rev. *Walter Harper*, Lecturer of St. *Andrew's, Holborn*.
John Hackett, Eſq; *Moor Hall, Sutton Coldfeild, Warw*.
Rev. *John Harriſon*, LL.B. Rector of *Wrabneſs, Eſſex*.
John Hancock Hall, LL. B. of *Trinity Hall, Cambridge*.
Rev. *Arth. Edw. Howman*, M.A. Rector of *Burſtow, Surry*.
1794 Rev. *Thomas Hey*, D. D. Prebendary of *Rocheſter*.
Rev. *Benj. Holmes*, B. D. Rector of *Freſhwater*, in the
    Iſle of *Wight*.
Rev. *James Hicks*, M.A. Rector of *Wiſtow, Huntingdonſh*.
Rev. *William Hett*, M. A. Prebendary of *Lincoln*.
Rev. *Wm. Hooper*, B. D. Fellow of *Univerſity* Coll. *Oxon*.
Charles Hoare, Eſq; *Fleet-ſtreet*.

I   Rev.

1794 Rev. *J. Hopkins*, M. A. Fellow of *Chriſt* Coll. *Camb.*
1795 Mr. *Wm. Holmes*, Merchant, of *Exeter.*
    Edw. Houghton, Eſq; *Liverpool.*
    Rev. *Andrew Hatt*, Curate of St. *Botolph, Aldgate.*
    Rev. *Ric. Harvey*, M. A. Curate of *Wingham, Kent.*
    Rev. *S. Henſhall*, M. A. Fellow of *Brazen Noſe* Coll. *Oxon.*
1796 Rev. *Joſeph Hordern*, M. A. *Royton*, near *Mancheſter.*
    Rev. *John Hallward*, M. A. Vicar of *Aſſington, Suffolk.*
    Rev. *Rob. Holmes*, D. D. Canon of *Chriſt Church, Oxon.*
    Tho. Hopkins, Eſq; *North Cerney Houſe*, near *Cirenceſter.*
    Rev. *J. Howe*, M. A. Rector of *Ridmerley Dabitot, Worc.*
    Rev. *Wm. Howley*, M. A. Fellow of *Winton* College.
    Joſeph Hornby, Eſq; *Kirkham, Lancaſhire.*
    Rev. *J Hutchins*, M. A. Rector of St. *Ann's, Alderſgate.*
    Rev. *Samuel Hornbuckle*, B. A. of C. C. C. *Cambridge.*
1797 *Henry Hobhouſe*, Eſq; *Middle Temple, London.*
    Rev. *Wm. Haggitt*, M. A. Chaplain of *Chelſea* Hoſp.
    Mr. *J. Hingeſton*, Jun. *Cheapſide, London.*
    Rev. *John Holmes*, B. A. *Gaudy Hall*, near *Harleſton, Norf.*
    Rev. *Ric. Hele*, B. D. Rector of *Rotherfeild Grays, Oxon.*
    Rev. *George Halton*, Rector of *Gate Burton.*
    Rev. *Robert Hodgſon*, M. A. Rector of *Laindon, Eſſex.*
1798 *Quarles Harris*, Jun. Eſq; of *Plaſkett, Eſſex.*
    Hon. and Rev. *Henry Lewis Hobart*, M. A Rector of
        Chippin Warden, Northamptonſhire.
    Gideon Hebert, Eſq; *Clement's Lane, Lombard Street.*
    Rev. *Gilbert Heathcote*, M. A. Fellow of *New* Coll.
        Oxford, and Vicar of *Collenne, Wilts.*
    Henry Hall, D. C. L. Fellow of St. *John's* Coll. *Oxford.*
    Rev. *Rob. Hankinſon*, M. A. *Trinity* College *Cambridge.*
1799 Rev. *Drake Hollingbury*, M. A. Chancellor of *Chicheſter.*
    Sir *J. D. Heſketh*, Bart. *Rufford, Lancaſhire.*
    Hugh Hammerſley, Eſq; of *Pall-mall.*

                                        Harrington

1799 *Harrington Hudfon*, Efq; of *Boffingby*, *Yorkfhire*.
Rev. *James Haviland*, M. A. Fellow of *New* Coll. *Oxf,*
Rev. *G. Haggitt*, M. A. Fellow of *Pembroke* Hall, *Camb*.
Rev. *Hamlet Harrifon*, M. A. Fellow of *Brazen Nofe* Coll.
   Oxford, and Mafter of *Brewood* School, *Stafford*.
Rev. *W. Heath*, M. A. Vicar of *Ficklarrow*, *Worcefterfh*.
Rev. *Wm. Hall*, M. A. Mafter of the Grammar School,
   at *Haydon Bridge*, *Northumberland*.
Rev. *R. Harvey*, Jun. Vicar of *St. Lawrence*, Ifle of *Thanet*.
John Huddleftone, Efq; *Down Place,Bray*, near *Maidenhead*.
Eufebius Horton, Efq; *Calton*, *Derbyfhire*.
Mr. *Geo. Hollingfworth*, *Darlington*, *Durham*.

I.

1768 R EV. *Simon Jacfon*, M. A. Rector of *Tarporley*, *Chefh*.
1772   Rev. *R. Ingram*, M. A. Vicar of *Wormingford*, *Effex*.
1774 Rev. *G. H. Purefoy Jervoife*, Rector of *Shalftone*, *Bucks*.
1777 Rev. *Wm. Johnfon*, M. A. *Purley Place*, near *Croydon*.
1778 Rev. *John Jenkins*, LL. B. Prebendary of *Wells*.
1779 *Richard Jenkyns*, Efq; *Wells*, *Somerfetfhire*.
1782 Rev. *Hugh Ingles*, D. D. Mafter of *Rugby* School.
1784 Rev. *J. Jaques*, M. A. Prebendary of *Lincoln*, and Rector
   of *Little Packington*, *Warwickfhire*.
Rev. *Lafcelles Iremonger*, M. A. Vicar of *Clatford*, *Hants*.
Rev. *Maurice Johnfon*, D. D. Prebendary of *Lincoln*,
   and Vicar of *Moulton*, *Lincolnfhire*.
1785 Rev. *Cyril Jackfon*, D. D. Dean of *Chrift Church*, *Oxon*.
Rev. *John Jones*, D. D. *Armagh*, *Ireland*.
1786 Rev. *Edw. Jones*, M. A. Rector of *Uppingham*, *Rutlandfh*.
1787 Rev. *John Jenner*, D. D. Rector of *Buckland*, *Kent*.
Rev. *Tho. Jeans*, M. A. Rector of *Witchingham*, *Norf*.
Rev. *Wm. Jones*, M. A. Rector of *Pafton*, *Northamp*.

5   Rev.

1787 Rev. *Wm. Jackson*, B.D. Canon of *Chrift Church, Oxon.*
Rev. *Thomas Ireland*, D.D. Prebendary of *Wells.*
Rev. *Croxton Johnson*, Rector of *Wilmflow, Chefhire.*
1788 Rev. *H. C. Jeffreys*, Rector of *Minching Hampton, Glouc.*
Rev. *Benj. Jeffreys*, M. A. Fellow of *Winton College.*
Rev. *Jofeph Jowett*, LL.D. Regius Profeffor of Civil
Law in the Univerfity of *Cambridge.*
1789 Mr. *John Jowett, Newington, Surry.*
1790 Rev. *James Jones*, D. D. Archdeacon of *Hereford.*
1791 Rev. *Henry Jones*, M. A. Vicar of *Shorne, Kent.*
Rev. *James Jones*, M. A. Vicar of *Cobham*, near *Rochefter.*
Thomas Johnson, Efq; *Manchefter.*
Rev. *William Jackson*, Vicar of *Chrift Church, Hants.*
1792 Rev. *Wm. Jenkins*, M. A. Rector of *Melbury, Dorfet.*
Rev. *Rob. Jones*, M.A. Fellow of St. *John's* Coll. *Camb.*
Rev. *Rowl. Ingram*, B.D. *Ipfwich.*
Rev. *Roger Jacfon*, M.A. Rector of *Bebington, Chefhire.*
1793 Rev. *Jeremiah Jackson*, M. A. Vicar of *Offpringe, Kent.*
1794 Rev. *R. A. Ingram*, B.D. Fellow of *Queen's* Coll. *Camb.*
Rev. *John Jones*, Vicar of St. *Dogwell's, Haverford-Weft.*
Rev. *Edm. Ifham*, D.D. Warden of *All Souls* Coll. *Oxon.*
Rev. *John Jephcott*, LL.B. Rect. of *Kiflingbury, Northamp.*
Rev. *Ric. Jackson*, M. A. Vicar of *Abergele, Denbighfh.*
John Chambers Jones, Efq; *Bryn Eifleddfod, Denbighfh.*
Rev. *Stiverd Jenkins*, Curate of *Hannington*, near *Newbury.*
Rev. *Cha. Johnfon*, Vicar of *South Stoke, Bath.*
1795 Rev. *John Jackson*, M. A. Rector of *Cheadle, Staffordfh.*
Rev. *Tho. James*, D. D. Prebendary of *Worcefter.*
1796 Rev. *Hugh Jones, Lewifham, Kent.*
George James, Efq; *Bruton-ftreet, Berkley-fquare.*
Rev. *R. Jarrett*, M. A. Vicar of *Wellington, Somerfet.*
Rev. *Wm. Jones*, B. A. Curate of *Lanwada, Carnarvonfh.*
1797 Rev. *John Jeffreys*, M. A. Rector of *Barnes, Surry.*
Fifher Jackfon, Efq; *Mile End, Stepney.*

H   Mr.

1799 Mr. *Richard Jofeph*, *Little New-ftreet.*
Rev. G. *Jenyns*, M. A. Vicar of *Swaffham Prior*, *Camb.*

K.

1787 **R**IGHT Honourable Earl of *Kinnoul.*
1762 Mr. *Robert Kelham*, *Hatton-Garden.*
1769 Rev. Sir *Richard Kaye*, Bart. LL.D. Dean of *Lincoln.*
1771 Rev. *Sam. Kettilby*, D.D. Vicar of St.*Bartholomew theLefs!*
1777 Rev. *Nicholas Kendall*, Vicar of *Newlyn*, *Cornwall.*
Rev. Sir *John Knightley*, Bart. Rector of *Byfield*,*Northamp.*
1780 *Benjamin Kenton*, Efq; *Gower-ftreet.*
1781 *J. Kerridge*, Efq; *Whitton White Houfe*, *Ipfwich.*
1783 *Guftavus Adolp. Kempenfelt*, Efq; *Berners-ftreet.*
1785 Rev. *Thomas Knowles*, D. D. Prebendary of *Ely.*
William Knox, Efq; *Soho Square.*
1786 Rev. *John Keyfall*, M. A. Rector of *Groton* in *Suffolk*,
and Chaplain in ordinary to his Majefty.
Rev. *J. Keble*, M. A. Vicar of *Coln St. Aldwin's*, *Gloc.*
Thomas Kynafton, Efq; *Witham Grove*, *Effex.*
1787 Rev. *Ric. King*, M. A. Rector of *Worthing*, *Salop.*
Rev. *Edw. Kilvington*, M.A. *Orlingbury*, *Northamptonfh.*
1788 Rev. *Tho. Kipling*, D.D. Vicar of *Holme*, *Spalding Moor*,
Yorkfhire.
1789 Rev. *Jarvis Kenrick*, Vicar of *Chilham* cum *Molafh*, *Kent.*
Mr. *Henry Kempfon*, *Birmingham.*
1790 *John Kingfton*, Efq; *Stratford-place.*
1791 Rev.*Hen.Knapp*,M.A.Rector of*Stoke-Albany*,*Northamp.*
1792 Rev. *Tho. Kerrick*, Rector of *Banham*, *Norfolk.*
Rev. *Rob. Knight*, M. A. Vicar of *Beyton*, near *Bewdley.*
Rev. *John Kelly*, LL.D. Vicar of *Ardley*, near.*Colchefter.*
Rev. *Sam. Kilderbee*, M.A. Rector of *Campfey Afh*, *Suffolk.*
1794 Rev. *F. F. Knottesford*, M.A. *Hadleigh*, *Suffolk.*

Tho.

1795 *Tho. Kilvington*, Efq; M. B. *Ripon, Yorkſhire.*
Rev. *R. H. Knight*, M. A. Rector of *WeſtonFavell, Northamp.*
Rev. *Henry Kett*, B. D. Fellow of *Trinity* Coll. *Oxford.*
1799 Rev. *Wm. Keyt*, M. A. Vicar of *Runcorn, Cheſhire.*

L.

1767 R Ight Rev. *Beilby*, Lord Biſhop of *London.*
1771 Hon. and Right Rev. *James*, Lord Biſhop of *Litch-*
field and *Coventry.*
1784 Right Rev. *Richard*, Lord Biſhop of *Llandaff.*
1787 Right Rev. *George*, Lord Biſhop of *Lincoln.*
1775 Right Rev. *Euſeby*, Lord Biſhop of *Leighlin* and *Fernes.*
1768 Rev. *John Law*, D. D. Archdeacon of *Rocheſter.*
Rev. *John Longe*, M. A. Rector of *Spixworth, Norfolk.*
1769 *Charles Lawſon*, M. A. Maſter of the Free Grammar-
School, at *Mancheſter.*
1770 Rev. *Philip Lyne*, LL. D. Vicar of *Mevagiſſey, Cornwall.*
Bennet Langton, Efq; *Langton, Lincolnſhire.*
1778 Rev. *Thomas Lyttelton, Wanſtead, Eſſex.*
1780 Rev. *William Langford*, D. D. Canon of *Windſor.*
1781 Rev. *J. S. Luſhington*, M. A. Vicar of *Newcaſtle upon Tyne.*
1782 Rev. *James Lyon*, M. A. Rector of *Preſtwich, Lancaſhire.*
Rev. *C. P. Layard*, D. D. Prebendary of *Worceſter*, and
Chaplain in Ordinary to his Majeſty.
1783 Rev. *J. Lipyeatt*, M. A. Rector of *Great Hallingbury, Eſſex.*
1784 Rev. *Thomas Lear*, M. A. Fellow of *Wincheſter* College.
Rev. *William Lord*, M. A. Prebendary of *Chicheſter*,
and Rector of *Northian, Suſſex.*
1785 Rev. *John Liptrott*, B. A. Rector of *Offham, Kent.*
Thomas Lane, Efq; *Coffleet*, near *Plympton, Devonſh.*
1786 Rev. *Alex. Longmore*, LL. B. Vicar of *Baddow, Eſſex.*
Ric. W. Lytton, Efq; *Enfield, Middleſex.*
1787 Rev. *John Lowe*, M. A. Vicar of *Brotherton, Yorkſhire.*
John Latham, M. D. *Bedford Row.*

1787 Rev. *Thomas Lambard*, Rector of *Aſh*, *Kent*.
Benjamin Lacam, Eſq; *Cecil ſtreet*.
Rev. *Wm. Layton*, M. A. Rector of S:. *Matthew's*, *Ipſw*.
1788 *John Lulham*, Eſq; of *Ryſlip*, *Middleſex*.
Rev. *John Lettice*, D. D. Vicar of *Peaſmarſh*, *Suſſex*.
Rev. *Wm. Leigh*, LL. B. Rector of *Little Plumſtead*, *Norf*.
Rev. *S. Langſton*, M. A. Rector of *Hulcot*, *Bucks*.
Rev. *Rob. Lucas*, D. D. Rector of *Ripple*, *Worceſterſh*.
John Loveday, LL. D. *Williamſcott*, *Banbury*.
Rev. *John Lake*, Rector of *Lanivet*, *Cornwall*.
Rev. *Rob. Loxham*, B. A. Rector of *Stickney*, *Lincolnſh*.
1789 Rev. *Thomas Leigh*, LL. B. Rector of *Broadwell* and
Adleſtrop, *Glouceſterſhire*.
Rev. *John Lyon*, Vicar of *St. Mary's*, *Dover*.
Rev. *J. Lea*, M. A. Rector of *Acton Burnell*, *Shrewſbury*.
1790 Rev. *Harry Lee*, M. A. Fellow of *Winton* College.
Rev. *John Land*, M. A. Rector of *Hemyock*, in *Devon*.
Rev. *John Lynch*, D. D. Archdeacon of *Canterbury*.
1791 *Daniel Lyſons*, M. D. *Bath*.
Rev. *Ric. Lendon*, M. A. Rector of St. *John's*, *Clerkenwell*.
Edward Lloyd, Eſq; *Cefn*, *Denbighſhire*.
1792 Rev. *Tho. Lloyd*, M. A. Fellow of *King's* Coll. *Camb*.
Rev. *Joſeph L. Littlehales*, LL. D. Rector of *Grendon
Underwood* and Vicar of *Brill* and *Borſtall*, *Bucks*.
Rev. *Ric. Lloyd*, M. A. Rector of *Midhurſt*, *Suſſex*.
Rev. *Marm. Lawſon*, Preb. of *Ripon*, and Rector of *Sproatley*.
1793 *John Ludford*, Eſq; LL. D. *Anſley Hall*, *Warwickſhire*.
Rev. *Oſwald Leyceſter*, Vicar of *Knutsford*, *Cheſhire*.
1794 *John Lloyd*, Eſq; *Staſodunos*, *Denbighſhire*.
Mr. *M. Longridge*, *Sunderland*, near the Sea, *Durham*.
1795 Mr. *John Langton*, of *Kirkham*, *Lancaſhire*.
Hon. and Rev. *Cha. Lindſay*, M. A. Rector of *Tidd St.
Giles*, in the *Iſle* of *Ely*.
Mr. *Ric. Langſton*, of *Mancheſter*.

Rev.

1796 Rev. *Evan Lloyd*, B.D. of *Orſett*, *Eſſex*.
R. *Lodge*, Eſq; of *Carliſle*, *Cumberland*.
Rev. *Peter Lathbury*, M.A. of *Woodbridge*, *Suffolk*.
Rev. *Thomas Leigh*, M.A. Rector of *Little Tey*, *Eſſex*.
1797 Rev. *Francis Lundy*, Rector of *Lockington*, near *Beverly*.
Rev. *Samuel Locke*, M.A. Curate of *Farnham*, *Hants*.
1798 Rev. *Clement Leigh*, B.A. of *Chriſt* Coll. *Camb*.
Rev. *John Longe*, M.A. Vicar of *Coddenham*, *Suffolk*.
Rev. *Tho. Lloyd*, Rector of *Abrighton*, near *Wolverhamp*.
Samuel Lichigarey, Eſq; *Phillybrook* Houſe, *Layton*, *Eſſex*,
Rev. *Benj. Lawrence*, M.A. Curate of *Marybone*.
1799 Rev. *Ric.Lucas*, M.A.Rector of *Caſterton Magna*, *Rutland*.
Rev. *Cha. Lucas*, M.A. Curate of *Avebury*, *Wilts*.
Rev. *Tho. LeMeſurier*, M.A. Fellow of *New* Coll. *Oxon*.
Edward Long, Eſq; of *Ealing*, *Middleſex*.
W. A. Latham, Eſq; *Upper Seymour-ſtreet*.

M.

1798 **M**OST Rev. *Thomas Lewis*, Lord Biſhop of *Meath*.
1797 Right Rev. Biſhop *Macfarlane*, *Inverneſs*, N.B.
1762 Rev. *Herbert Mayo*, D.D. Rector of St. *George* in the
Eaſt, *Middleſex*.
1763 Rev. *John Moore*, LL.B. Rector of St. *Michael Baſſiſhaw*.
1771 Rev. *Stephen Moore*, M.A. Prebendary of *York*, and
Vicar of *Doncaſter*, *Yorkſhire*.
1772 Rev. *Richard Moſely*, Rector of *Drinkſton*, *Suffolk*.
Wm. B. Maſſingberd, Eſq; of *South Ormbeſby*, *Linc*.
1773 Rev. *Charles Moſs*, M.A. Archdeacon of St.*David's*.
1775 Sir *Charles Middleton*, Bart. M.P. *Hartford-ſtreet*.
1779 Rev. *Rob. Morres*, M.A. Vicar of *Britford*, near *Sarum*.
1780 Rev. *John Mayor*, B.A. Vicar of *Shawbury*, *Salop*.
Rev. *Tho. Mantell*, M.A. Fellow of C. C. C. *Camb*.

Wm.

1782 *Wm. Marwood,* Efq; *Bufby-Hall,* near *Stokefley, York W.*
1783 Rev. *William Morice,* D. D. Rector of *Allhallows,*
    Bread-ftreet, and Chaplain in Ordinary to His Majefty.
1784 Rev. *John Myers,* M. A. Rector of *Wyberton, Lincolnfh.*
1785 Rev. *Ric. Mant,* D. D. Rector of *All Saints, Southampton.*
    Rev. *Mic. Marlow,* D.D. Prefident of St. *John's Coll. Oxon.*
1786 Rev. *Wm. Manley,* Rector of *Stoke-Fleming, Devon.*
    Major *Archibald Mitchell,* in the Service of the *Eaft-
    India* Company,
    Rev. *John Moffop,* Vicar of *Bafton, Lincolnfhire.*
    Rev. *Tho. Marfham,* M.A. Rector of *Alwalton, Hunts.*
    Rev. *Tho. Moore,* M. A. Rector of *North Cray.*
    John Marratt, Efq; *Dedham, Effex.*
1787 Rev. *L. Mercier,* Minifter of the *French* London Church.
    James Mann, Efq; *Linton, Kent.*
    Rev. *Tho. Mills,* Vicar of *Hillingdon, Middlefex.*
1788 *Lewis Majendie,* Efq; *Hedingham* Caftle, *Effex.*
    Rev. *Spencer Madan,* M. A. Canon Refid. of *Litchfield.*
    Henry Euftace M'Culloh, Efq; *Lincoln's-inn-fields.*
    Rev. *Cha. Mofs,* D.D. Canon Refidentiary of St. *Paul's.*
    Rev. *Cha. S. Miller,* M. A. Vicar of *Harlow, Effex.*
    Fiennes S. Miller, Efq; of *Radway, Warwickfhire.*
    Rev. *Wm. Myers, North Somercotes, Lincolnfhire.*
    Rev. *Geo. Marfh,* M. A. *Long-Critchill, Dorfet.*
1789 *Job Matthew,* Efq; *Woodford.*
    Rev. *Tho. Mogg,* Vicar of *High Littleton, Somerfet.*
    Wm. Marriot, Efq; *Perfhore, Worcefterfhire.*
    Rev. *Rob. Myddelton,* D.D. Rector of *Rotherbithe.*
    Rev. *Rob. Miller,* LL.B. Vicar of St. *Nicholas, Warwick.*
    John May, Efq; of *Hoborough,* near *Rochefter.*
    Rev. *John Maule,* M. A. Chaplain of *Greenwich Hofpital.*
1790 *William Morland,* Efq; *Pall-mall.*
    Rev. *Cha. Mayo,* B. D. Fellow of St. *John's Coll. Oxf.*

        4   Rev.

1791 Rev.*W.H.Majendie*, D.D. Canon Refidentiary of *St. Paul's.*
      Rev. *H. Morgan,* M.A. Canon Refidentiary of *Hereford.*
      Richard Moore, Efq; *Long Melford, Suffolk.*
1792 Rev. *John Middleton,* M.A. Rector of *Willesford, Linc.*
      Rev. *W. Maffingberd,* Rector of *South Ormfby, Linc.*
      Rev. *George Markham,* M. A. Chancellor of *York.*
      Rev. *I. H. Michell,* M.A. Fellow of *King's* Coll. *Camb.*
      Rev. *John Meffeter,* M.A. Rector of *Brallon, Somerfetfh.*
      Rev. *Chriftopher Moor,* Vicar of *Lilbourn, Northamptonfh.*
1793 Rev. *H. Meen,* M. A. Rector of *St. Nicholas, Cole-Abby.*
      Rev. *Tho. Hooper Morrifon,* B. A. *New* College, *Oxon.*
      Rev. *Edw. Mills,* M. A. Preacher at *Bury St. Edmonds.*
      Mr. *Jofeph Manning, Orlingbury, Northamptonfhire.*
      Rev. *Rob. Mefhem,* M.A. Fellow of *Jefus* College, *Oxon.*
1794 Rev. *John Manwaring,* B. D. Margaret Profeffor of
      Divinity, in the Univerfity of *Cambridge.*
      Rev. *F. Maffingberd,* M.A. Rector of *Wafhingbrough, Linc.*
      Rev. *Edw. Maltby,* M. A. Vicar of *Buckden, Hunts.*
      Rev. *Geo. Moore,* M. A. Archdeacon of *Cornwall.*
      Sam. Mills, Efq; *Middle Moorfields.*
      Rev. *Wm. Mairis,* M.A. Vicar of *Bifhop's Lydeard, Somerf.*
1795 Rev. *Edw. Mellifh,* M. A. Vicar of *Honingham,* near *Norw.*
      Rev. *Edw. Miller,* Vicar of *All Saints, Northampton.*
      Rev. *John Marfhall,* Rector of *Wincombe, Oxon.*
      Rev. *J. Molefworth,* M.A. Rector of *St. Brock, Cornwall.*
      P. C. Methuen, Efq; *Lower Grofvenor-ftreet.*
1796 Rev. *Henry Milner,* LL.D. Rector of *Denton, Bucks.*
      Ezekiel Mackilwain, Efq; *Lymington, Hants.*
      Rev. *Wm. L. Manfell,* D.D. Mafter of *Trinity* Coll. *Camb.*
      George May, Efq; *Hearne,* near *Canterbury.*
      Ambrofe Martin, Efq; *Finch Lane.*
      Rev. *Cha. Mayfon,* D. D. Rector of *Lezant, Cornwall.*
1797 Rev. *Robert Markham,* M.A. Archdeacon of *York.*

                                              Francis

[64]

1797 *Francis Markett*, Efq; *Luddefdown*, near *Rochefter*.
Rev. *J. Morres*, M.A. Rector of *Nether-Broughton, Leicefl.*
1798 Rev. *T. C. May*, *Bremore*, *Hants*.
Rev. *J. B. Moulding*, B.D. Fellow of Trinity Coll. *Oxf.*
William Manning, Efq; M.P. *Totteridge*, *Herts*.
Rev. *Thomas Mears*, M.A. Rector of St. *Lawrence*, *cum*
   St. *John's Southampton*.
Rev. *Giles Meech*, B.A. Rector of *Compton-Abbas*, *Dorfet*.
Rev. *John White Middelton*, B.A. of *Trinity* Coll. *Oxford*.
Rev. *C. P. Myddleton*, M.A. Curate of St. *Mary's Manchef.*
Rev. *John Maule*, B.A. *Merton* College, *Oxford*.
1799 Mr. *John Mofer*, of *Prith-ftreet*, *Soho*.
John May, Efq; *Bedford-fquare*.
Rev. *Streynfham Mafter*, M.A. Rector of *Crofton*, *Lanc.*
Rev. *E. Mafter*, B.A. Rector of *Rufford*, *Lancafhire*.
Charles Tyrrel Morgan, Efq; *Fairford*, *Gloucefterfhire*.
Rev. *John Morgan*, B.D. Rector of *Chelmsford*, *Effex*.
George Milner, Efq; *Comberton*, near *Cambridge*.
John Maddifon, Efq; *Louth*, *Lincolnfhire*.
Rev. *Thomas Martyn*, B.D. Profeffor of Botany in the
   Univerfity of *Cambridge*.

N.

1794 RIGHT Rev. *Charles*, Lord Bifhop of *Norwich*.
1787 Right Rev. *Charles*, Bifhop of *Nova-Scotia*.
1761 Sir *Roger Newdigate*, Bart. of *Arbury*, *Warwickfh.*
1763 Rev. *Richard Neate*, LL.B. *Whetftone*, *Middlefex.*
1766 Rev. *John Napleton*, D.D. Canon Refid. of *Hereford.*
1768 Rev. *Rob. B. Nickolls*, LL.B. Dean of *Middleham*, *Yorkfh.*
1773 Rev. *Tho. Nowell*, D.D. Principal of St. *Mary* Hall, *Oxon.*
1775 Rev. *Anthony Natt*, Rector of *Nettefwell*, *Effex.*

6

Rev

1781 Rev. *Ric. Nicoll,* D. D. Rector of *Drayton, Oxfordfh.*
1782 Rev. *J. Norman,* B.D. Rector of *Kibworth, Leiceft.*
1784 Rev. *Nutcombe Nutcombe,* LL.B. Chancellor of the
      Church of *Exeter.*
1786 Rev. *Wm. Nelfon,* M. A. Rector of *Hilborough, Norf.*
1787 Rev. *John Nairn,* M.A. Rector of *Kingfton, Kent.*
      Rev. *R. Nares,* M.A. Canon Refidentiary of *Litchfield.*
1788 Rev. *Tho. Newton,* M. A. Rector of *Tewing, Herts.*
1789 Rev. *John Norbury,* D.D. Fellow of *Eton* College.
1793 Rev. *John North,* M. A. Rector of *Afhdon, Effex.*
      Rev. *S. C. Niffer,* Chaplain to the *Swedifh* Embaffy,
      and Rector of the *Swedifh* Lutheran Church in *London.*
1794 *Jacob Neufville,* Efq; *Lymington, Hants.*
      Rev. *Hen. H. Norris,* M.A. *Hackney, Middlefex.*
      Rev. *Geo. Nicholas,* LL.D. Mafter of *Ealing* School, *Midd.*
1796 *George Nicholls,* Efq; *Milton, Cambridgefhire.*
1798 *John Nott,* Efq; *Swymbridge,* near *Barnftaple, Devonfh.*
      Jofiah Nottidge, Efq; *Bocking, Effex.*
      Rev. *Thomas Neate,* B. A. *Battle, Suffex.*
1799 Rev. *G. F. Nott,* M. A. Fellow of *All Souls* Coll. *Oxford.*
      Rev. *James Newton,* Curate of *Weft Kirby, Chefhire.*

O.

1784 R Ight Reverend *John,* Lord Bifhop of *Oxford.*
1758   Rev. *Newton Ogle,* D. D. Dean of *Winchefter.*
1769 Rev. *Edw. Owen,* M. A. Rector of *Warrington, Lanc.*
1777 Rev. *Arthur Onflow,* D. D. Dean of *Worcefter.*
1785 *James Oakes,* Efq; *Bury St. Edmund's.*
1786 Rev. *Ric. Ormerod,* M.A. Vicar of *Kenfington, Middlefex.*
      Rev. *J. Owen,* B.A. late Chap.to the Prefidency of *Bengal.*
1790 Rev. *James Ogilvie,* D. D. Chaplain at his Majefty's
      Lodge in *Windfor* Great Park.
      William Orde, Efq; *Morpeth, Northumberland.*
      Rev. *Harry Oglander,* B. D. Fellow of *Winton* College.
                    I   Rev.

1791 Rev. *Thomas Orme*, D. D. Mafter of the Grammar-School of *Louth, Lincolnfhire.*
1792 Rev. *N. T. Orgile*, M. A. Rector of *Worlingham, Suffolk.*
Rev. *John Oldham*, M. A. Rector of *Standen, Effex.*
1795 Rev. *John Ord*, D. D. Rector of *Burgh St. Mary's, Norf.*
1796 Rev. *Daniel Olivier*, LL. B. Rector of *Clifton, Bedfordfh.*
1797 Rev. *Owen Owen*, M. A. of *Fynnogion* near *Ruthin, Denb.*

P.

1790 **R**Ight Rev. *Spencer*, Lord Bifhop of *Peterborough*.
1750   Rev. *John Peele*, M. A. Vicar of St. *Peter's, Norwich.*
1755 Rev. *Charles Poyntz*, D. D. Prebendary of *Durham.*
1761 Rev. *William Paley, Gigglefwick, Yorkfhire.*
1764 Rev. *William Pemberton*, M. A. Rector of *Rufhbury, Salop.*
1765 *William Poyntz*, Efq; *Midgham, Berks.*
1766 *Edm. Pepys*, Efq; *Upper Charlotte-ftreet.*
1769 Rev. *Wm. Parker*, D. D. Rector of St. *James's, Weftminfter.*
1770 Rev. *William Polhill*, Rector of *Albury, Surry.*
1771 Rev. *Samuel Peach*, M. A. *Eaft Sheen, Surry.*
1772 Rev. *Baptift Proby*, D. D. Dean of *Litchfield*, and Rector of *Doddington*, in the Ifle of *Ely.*
Rev. *Henry Poole, Chaily, Suffex.*
1776 Rev. *William Paley*, D. D. Sub-Dean of *Lincoln.*
1777 *Clopton Prbys*, Efq; *Llandrinio, Montgomeryfhire.*
Wilfon Pearfon, Efq; *Bridekirk, Cumberland.*
Rev. *Tho. Pearce*, D. D. Prebendary of *Chefter*, and Sub-Dean of His Majefty's *Chapels Royal.*
1780 Rev. *Wm. Phelips*, Rector of *Cucklington, Somerfet.*
1781 Rev. *Ric. Perryn*, M. A. Rector of *Standifh, Wigan.*
Peter Perchard, Efq; Alderman of *London.*
1782 *Samuel Prime*, Efq; *Upper Broak-Street.*
Charles Palmer, Efq; *Bifrons, Wanftead, Effex.*
1783 Rev. *Hugh Price*, M. A. Rector of *Rettendon, Effex.*
1784 Mr. Deputy *Pickwoad, Cloak-lane.*

Rev.

1784 Rev. *John Penroſe*, Rector of *Fledborough, Nottinghamſh.*
1785 Rev. *Joſ. Plymley*, M.A. Archdeacon of *Salop, Hereford.*
1786 Rev. *William E. Page*, M.A. Vicar of *Frodſham, Cheſh.*
Rev. *Wm. Pares*, LL.B. Vicar of *Selſton, Nottinghamſh.*
Rev. *Rob. Price*, LL.D. Canon of *Saliſbury.*
Rev. *John Prower*, Vicar of *Purton, Wilts.*
Hon. *Philip Puſey, Upper Groſvenor-ſtreet.*
Mr. *Joſiah Patrick, Crowneſt, Worceſter.*
Rev. *Wollaſton Pym*, M.A. Rector of *Radwell, Herts.*
Ralph Peters, Eſq; *Platbridge*, near *Wigan.*
1787 Rev. *Cha. Platt*, B.D. *Forthampton*, near *Tewkeſbury.*
Rev. *James Pope*, B.D. Vicar of *Great Stoughton, Hunts.*
Rev. *Harry Paxton*, M.A.
Rev. *John Pridden*, M.A. Minor Canon of St. *Paul's.*
1788 Mr. *John Pares, Leiceſter.*
Rev. *James Phillott*, D.D. Archdeacon and Rector of *Bath.*
Rev. *Ric. Purdy*, B.D. Vicar of *Cricklade, Wilts.*
William Preſcott, Eſq; *Clapham.*
Rev. *Sam. Partridge*, M.A. Vicar of *Boſton, Linc.*
1789 Rev. *Wm. Pearce*, D.D. Dean of *Ely.*
Edward Palmer, Eſq; *Birmingham.*
Rev. *E. Palmer*, Vicar of *Stoke Gurſey, Somerſet.*
Mr. *Theodore Price, Birmingham.*
John Prieſtley, Eſq; *Lodge*, near *Hallifax.*
Rev. *James Pinnock*, M.A. Rector of *Laſham, Hants.*
F. Pym, Eſq; *Haſells-Hall*, in *Sandy, Bedfordſh.*
1790 Rev. *Rob. Pierſon*, M.A. Archdeacon of *Cleveland.*
James Allan Park, Eſq; Vice-Chancellor of the County-Palatine of *Lancaſter.*
Henry Parker, Eſq; *Stoke-Newington, Middleſex.*
Rev. *Joſ. H. Pott*, M.A. Archdeacon of *St. Alban's.*
Rev. *John Prince*, B.A. Chaplain to the *Magdalen Hoſp.*
Rev. *J. D. Pleſtow*, B.D. Rector of *Watlington, Norf.*
Rev. *T. Parkinſon*, D.D. Archdeacon of *Huntingdon.*

I 2   Rev.

1790 Rev. *R. Pointer*, M. A. Rector of *Broughton, Huntingdonfh.*
1791 *Thomas Pares*, Jun. Efq; *Leicefter.*
 Rev. *Henry Parfons*, M. A. Prebendary of *Wells*, and Rector of *Goathurft, Somerfet.*
 Rev. *James Price*, M. A. Vicar of *High Wycombe.*
 Theophilus Pritzler, Efq; *Wellclofe-fquare.*
 Rev. *Phineas Pett*, B. D. Rector of *Chilbolton, Hants.*
1792 Rev. *Jof. Price*, B. D. Vicar of *Littlebourne, Kent.*
 Rev. *John Papillon*, Vicar of *Tunbridge, Kent.*
 Mr. *Thomas Pearfon*, of *Birmingham.*
 Mr. *James Prefton*, of *Hounflow.*
 Rev. *G. Prefton*, M. A. Rect. of *Beefton St. Lawrence, Norf.*
 Rev. *Ed. Pearfon*, B. D. Rector of *Rempfton, Notts.*
 Rev. *John Pedder*, B. A. *Lancafter.*
 Rev. *Wm. Portal*, B. D. Rector of *Wafing*, near *Reading.*
 Rev. *Reginald Pyndar*, *Hadfor, Worcefterfhire.*
 Rev. *Tho. Prefton*, M. A. *Moorby, Yorkfhire.*
1793 Rev. *Matt. Pewley*, Vicar of *Dewfbury*, near *Wakefield.*
 Rev. *R. Porteus*, M. A. Rector of *Bifhop's Wickham, Effex.*
 Rev. *Jofeph Pomery*, M. A. Vicar of *St. Kew, Cornwall.*
 Rev. *John Penfold*, Vicar of *Steyning, Suffex.*
 Rev. *John Parkinfon*, M. A. Rector of *Healing, Linc.*
 Rev. *Edw. Parry*, Vicar of *Bettws, Montgomeryfh.*
 Rev. *John Plumtree*, M. A. Prebendary of *Worcefter.*
 Rev. *Rice Pughe*, Rector of *Llysfuen, Carnarvonfhire.*
1795 Rev. *Cha. Proby*, M. A. Rector of *Stanwick, Northampt.*
 Henry Hinde Pelly, Efq; *Upton, Weft Ham, Effex.*
 William Price, Efq; Vice Chamberlain to her Majefty.
 Rev. *T. Percy*, LL. D. Fellow of St. *John's* Coll. *Oxon.*
 Rev. *Wm. Parker*, M. A.
 Rev. *H. Powell*, LL. B. Rector of *Eaft Horndon, Effex.*
 Rev. *H. J. Parker*, M. A. Curate of *Tooting, Surry.*
1796 Rev. *G. L. Perry*, B. A. of St. *John's* Coll. *Oxford.*
 David Powell, jun. Efq; *Little St. Helen's, London.*

          John

1796 *John Peachy,* Efq; *Hornet,* near *Chichefter.*
   Rev. —— *Pickering,* Rector of *Bifhop's Cleve, Glocefterfh.*
   Rev. *Wm. Pigott,* Rector of *Edgermond, Salop.*
   Rev. *John Palmer,* M. A. Fellow of St. *John's* Coll. *Camb.*
1797 *Thomas M. Phillips,* Efq; *More Critchill, Dorfet.*
   Rev. *Wm. Parry,* M. A. Warden of *Ruthin, Denbigfh.*
   Rev. *Thomas Powys,* D. D. Dean of *Canterbury.*
   Edward Parry, Efq; *Gower Street, Bedford Square.*
   Rev. *Ric. Proffer,* D. D. Rector of *Gatefhead, Durham.*
   Rev. *R. B. Podmore,* M. A. Vicar of *Monks Kirby, Warw.*
1798 Mr. *Nath. Planner, Newington Butts, Surry.*
   Hon. *Charles Paget,* Captain in the Royal Navy.
   Rev. *Thomas Pennington,* Vicar of *Billefby, Lincolnfh.*
   John Puget, Efq; *John Street, Bedford Row.*
   Rev. *Charles Poole,* B. A. *Bridgewater, Somerfetfhire.*
   Sir *Edward Pellew,* Bart. Captain in the Royal Navy.
   Rev. *John Prowett,* M. A. Fellow of *New* Coll. *Oxford.*
1799 Rev. *Delabere Pritchett,* Fellow of *Trinity* Coll. *Camb.*
   Samuel Woodford Paul, Efq; *Lincoln's-Inn.*
   Rev. *L. Panting,* M. A. Minifter of *South Lambeth* Chapel.
   Rev. *Cha. Peters,* M. A. Fellow of *Queen's* Coll. *Oxford.*
   Rev. *Barrè Phipps,* B. A. Curate of *Poling, Suffex.*
   Thomas Poynder, Efq; *Clapham, Surry.*
   Rev. *Thomas Parke,* M. A. Rector of *Strethern, Leicefterfh.*
   Rev. *Wm. Palmer,* B. A. Curate of St. *Mary's, Reading.*

Q.

1790 RIGHT Rev. *Jacob,* Lord Bifhop of *Quebec.*

R.

1787 R Ight Rev. *Samuel,* Lord Bifhop of *Rochefter.*
1776   Right Hon. Earl of *Radnor.*
1752 Rev. *J. Riland,* M. A. Rector of *Sutton Coldfield, Warwick.*

1775 Rev. *Samuel Rogers*, M.A. Student of *Chrift Church, Oxon.*
1776 Rev. *Houftonne Radcliffe*, D.D. Prebendary of *Canterbury.*
1779 Rev. *Herb. Randolph*, B. D. Vicar of *Canewdon, Effex.*
1780 *Thomas Rafhleigh*, Efq; *Hatton-Garden.*
Jeffe Ruffell, Efq; *Goodman's-yard, Whitechapel.*
1785 Rev. *Jofeph J. Rye*, M.A. Vicar of *Dallington, Northampt.*
Rev. *Rich. Raikes*, M. A. Prebendary of St. *Paul's.*
1787 Rev. *Peter Rafhleigh*, M.A. Rector of *South Fleet, Kent.*
Mr. *Thomas Ridding, Southampton.*
1788 Rev. *Tho. Rennell*, D. D. Mafter of the *Temple.*
Rev. *Jas. Round*, M.A. Rector of St. *Runwald, Colchefter.*
Rev. *Matthias Rutton*, M.A. Vicar of *Sheldwick, Kent.*
1789 Mr. *Jofeph Rabone.*
Mr. *George Roadley, Whitecrofs-ftreet.*
Rev. *Rob. Ruffel*, M. A. Rector of *Ewhurft* and Vicar
of *Boddam, Suffex.*
Rev. *John Ridghill*, M.A. Rector of *Welburn, Lincolnfh.*
Thomas Raikes, Efq; *New Broad-ftreet.*
Rev. *Durand Rhudde*, D. D. Rector of *Eaft Burgholt, Suff.*
1790 *John Ranby*, Efq; *Sudbury, Suffolk.*
Rev. *Francis Randolph*, D. D. Prebendary of *Briftol.*
Rev. Sir *Ch. Rich*, Bart. LL.D. *Grove-place, Southampton.*
1791 Rev. *Tho. Roberts*, M.A. Rector of *Llangybly, Carnarv.*
Mr. *Robert Raikes, Gloucefter.*
Rev. *Ric. Ramfden*, M.A. Fellow of *Trinity* Coll. *Camb.*
1792 Rev. *Cha. Ruffel*, M. A. Minifter of *Wimborne, Dorfet.*
Rev. *William Roberts, Ceidio, Carnarvonfhire.*
Rev. *Wm. Roberts*, M. A. Fellow of *Eton* College.
Rev. *Ric. Rous*, Vicar of *Clift St. George, Devon.*
Rev. *Wm. L. Rofe*, M.A. Rector of *Whilton*, near *Daventry.*
Rev. *John Riley*, M. A. Rector of *Fobbing, Effex.*
1793 *Wm. Raikes*, Efq; *Alderman's Walk.*
Rev. *Tho. Rackett*, M. A. Rector of *Shetlifbury, Gloceflerfh.*
Rev. *John M. Rogers*, LL.B. Rector of *Perkeley, Somerfet.*

William

1793. *William Roberts*, Eſq; *Oakland*, near *Llanwrſt*, *Denbigh*.
 Rev. *Bertrand Ruſſel*, M. A. Vicar of *Gainford*, *Durham*.
 Rev. *Peter A. Reaſton*, M.A. Rect. of *Barlborough*, *Derbyſh*.
1794 Rev. *John Roberts*, B.D. Rector of *Keddington*, *Oxon*.
1795 Rev. *R. Rogers*, B. A. Curate of St. *Martin's in the Fields*.
1796 Rev. *Alex. Richardſon*, M.A. Fellow of *C. C. C. Camb.*
 Rev. *Edw. Robſon*, M. A. Vicar of *Orſton*, *Notts*.
1797 Rev. *Robert Roughſedge*, M.A. Rector of *Liverpool*.
 Rev. *John Robinſon*, B. A. Rector of *Ulceby*, *Lincolnſh*.
 Francis Reed, Eſq; *Hurworth*, *Durham*.
 William Rawſon, Eſq; *Halifax*, *Yorkſhire*.
 Rev. *James Reeve*, M. A. Curate of *Maidſtone*, *Kent*.
1798 *John Richardſon*, Eſq; of *Lincoln's Inn*
 Rev. *James Rodwell*, M. A. Head Maſter of the Grammar School at *Kingſton upon Hull*.
 Rev. *Legh Richmond*, M. A. Curate of *Brading*, in the *Iſle of Wight*.
 Rev. *T. C. Rudſton*, M. A. Curate of *Worthill*, near *York*.
 Rev. *William Roſe*, M. A. Rector of *Beckenham*, *Kent*.
 Hon. Sir *Giles Rooke*, Knt. one of the Judges of His Majeſty's Court of *Common Pleas*.
1799 Rev. *Tho. Robinſon*, M. A. Vicar of St. *Mary's*, *Leiceſter*.
 Mr. *John Rutter*, of *Love Lane*, *Aldermanbury*.
 Rev. *C. Richards*, M. A. Vicar of St. *Bartholomew Hide*, *Winc.*
 Rev. *Geo. Richards*, *Newport*, in the *Iſle of Wight*.
 James Robinſon, Eſq; *Papplewick*, *Nottinghamſhire*.
 Edward Riley, Eſq; *Hamſtall Ridivare*, *Stafford*.

S.

1779 R IGHT Rev. *John*, Lord Biſhop of *Saliſbury*.
1784   Right Rev. *Claudius*, Lord Biſhop of *Sodor* and *Mann*.

Right.

1773 Right Honourable Earl of *Stamford.*
1785 Right Honourable Earl *Spencer.*
1749 Rev. *Dye Syer,* D. D. Rector of *Kiddington, Suffolk.*
1762 *John Spiller,* Esq; *Brentford.*
1763 Rev. *Thomas Stevens,* M. A. Rector of *Bradfield, Berks.*
1765 *Francis Smyth,* Esq; *New Buildings, Yorkshire.*
1766 Rev. *Richard Shepherd,* D. D. Archdeacon of *Bedford.*
1767 *William Strode,* Esq; *Upper Brook-street.*
      John Stackhouse, Esq; *Pendarves, Cornwall.*
      Rev. *Charles Sturges,* M. A. Rector of *Chelsea.*
1768 Rev. *Samuel Smallbroke,* D. D. Rector of *Wem, Salop.*
1771 *Henry Southby,* Esq; *Bath.*
      William Stevens, Esq; Treasurer to Queen *Anne's* Bounty.
1772 Rev. *Tho. Stevens,* D. D. Rector of *Panfield, Essex.*
      Richard Spiller, Esq; *Bentinck Street, Cavendish Square.*
      Sir *William Scott,* Knt. LL. D. *Doctors Commons.*
      Rev. *Geo. P. Scobell,* Vicar of *Sancreed* and *St. Just, Cornw.*
1775 Rev. *John Sturges,* LL. D. Prebendary of *Winchester,*
      and Chancellor of the Diocese.
1776 Rev. *Samuel Strong,* Rector of *Marchwiel, Wrexham.*
      Rev. *Hen. Shepherd,* Rector of *Brandsburton, Holderness.*
      Rev. *Wm. Somerville,* M. A. Vicar of *Bibury* in *Glocest.*
1780 Rev. *M. S. Smith,* B. D. Rector of *Fladbury, Worcestersh.*
      John Seale, Esq; *Mount Boon,* near *Dartmouth, Devon.*
1781 Rev. *Samuel Swire,* B. D. Rector of *Melsonby, Yorkshire.*
1782 Rev. *Tho. Starkie,* M. A. Vicar of *Blackburn, Lanc.*
      Rev. *J. G. Smyth,* B. A. Curate of St. *Gregory, Norwich.*
      Rev. *John Sibley,* M. A. Rector of *Walcot,* near *Bath.*
1783 Rev. *James Stovin,* M. A. Rector of *Rossington, Doncaster.*
      Jacob Smith, Esq; *Wallsall, Staffordshire.*
      Rev. *Peter Sandiford,* M. A. Rector of *Fulmodestone, Norf.*
1784 Rev. *Henry Sawbridge,* Rector of *Welford, Berks.*
      Rev. *John K. Shaw Brooke,* M. A. Vicar of *Elkham, Kent.*
1785 Rev. *Samuel Sewell,* M. A. Vicar of *Prescot, Lancashire.*
                         Rev.

1785 Rev. *Cha. Sutton*, B.D. Rector of *Albergh, Norfolk*.
Rev. *Matt. Snow*, M.A. Rector of *Wakerly, Northamp.*
Rev. *William Speare, Exeter.*
Rev. *Humphrey Shuttleworth*, Vicar of *Prefton, Lanc.*
Rev. *Cha. Symmons*, D.D. Rector of *Narberth, Pemb.*
Mr. *Nathan Smith, Artillery Place, Brighton.*
1786 Rev. *John Simpfon*, Rector of *Roofs, Holdernefs.*
Rev. *Bence Sparrow*, Rector of *Beccles, Suffolk.*
Right Hon. Sir *John Skynner*, Knt. *Great George Street, Hanover Square.*
1787 Rev. *Cha. Sandiford*, M.A. Vicar of *Awre, Gloucef.*
Rev. *John Selwyn*, LL.B. Rector of *Luggerfhall, Wilts.*
Rev. *Hen. Sifmore*, LL.B. Fellow of *New* Coll. *Oxon.*
Rev. *John Smith*, M.A. Rector of *Bredon, Worcefterfh.*
Rev. *John Sheppard*, M.A. Curate of *Paddington, Middx.*
Rev. *Samuel Smith*, LL.D. Prebendary of *Weftminfter.*
Rev. *Jelinger Symons*, B.D. Rector of *Whitburne, Durh.*
Rev. *Richard Salmon*, Vicar of *Sandbach, Chefhire.*
1788 Rev. *John Simons*, LL.B. Rector of St. *Paul's Cray, Kent.*
Mr. *Thomas Slack, Diftaff-lane.*
Rev. *John Smith*, Rector of *Pattifley* and Vicar of *Matifhall, Norfolk.*
Timothy Shelley, Efq; M.A. of *Univ.* Coll. *Oxon.*
1789 Rev. *Tho. Sikes*, M.A. Vicar of *Guilfborough, Northampt.*
Mr. *George Simcox, Birmingham.*
Sir *James Saumarez*, Knt. Ifland of *Guernfey.*
Rev. *James Simons*, B.A. Rector of St. *Stephen's, Exon.*
Jofeph Sibley, Efq; *Northampton.*
Rev. *William Strong*, M.A. Archdeacon of *Northampt.*
1790 Rev. *R. D. Shackleford*, D.D. Vicar of *St. Sepulchre's.*
Drummond Smith, Efq; *Tring Park, Herts.*
Rev. *Tho. Ab. Salmon*, M.A. Prebendary of *Wells*, and Rector of *Rodney Stoke, Somerfetfhire.*

K   *Ric.*

1791 *Ric. Brook Supple*, Efq; *Great Oakley, Northamptonfh.*

Mr. *John Swann*, Surgeon, *Ollerton, Notts.*

Rev. *Rob. Sheffield*, M.A. Rector of *Flixborough, Lincolnfh.*

Rev. *James Stillingfleet*, M.A. Prebendary of *Worcefter.*

Rev. *Fr. Simpfon*, B.D. Rector of *Tarrant Gunville, Dorfet.*

Rev. *F. Swann*, *Lincoln.*

Rev. *Cha. Sloman*, LL.B. Vicar of *Eling, Hants.*

1792 Rev. *Matt. Surtees*, M.A. Rector of *North Cerney, Glouc.*

Rev. *Henry Stevens*, LL.B. *Bradfield, Berkfhire.*

Sam. Smith, Efq; M.P. *George-ftreet, Weftminfter.*

Rev. *Matt. Skinner*, M.A. of *Richmond, Surry.*

Rev. *Wm. Sandys*, M.A. Rector of St. *Minver, Cornwall.*

Rev. *John Sharpe*, Lecturer of *Clapham.*

1793 Rev. *Edward Smedley*, M.A. Vicar of *Meopham, Kent.*

Sir *John Gregory Shaw*, Bart. *Eltham, Kent.*

Richard Smart, Efq; *Lamb's Conduit Street.*

Rev. *Hen. Shield*, M.A. Rector of *Stoke Dry, Rutlandfh.*

Hen. Collingwood Selby, Efq; *Gray's-inn-fquare.*

Rev. *Benj. W. Salmon*, M.A. Rector of *Cafton, Norfolk.*

Rev. *Dav. Stodart*, M.A. Rector of *Llanderfel, Merioneth.*

Mr. *Benj. Smith*, of *Falkingham, Lincolnfhire.*

Richard Saumarez, Efq; *Newington, Surry.*

1794 Rev. *Rob. Shield*, M.A. Vicar of *Royfton, Herts.*

Rev. *Humphry Smythies*, M.A. Rector of *Alpheton, Suff.*

Rev. —— *Shelton*, Vicar of *Overbury, Worcefterfhire.*

Sir *Chrift. Sykes*, Bart. LL.D. of *Sledmere, Yorkfhire.*

Rev. *Ja. Simpkinfon*, M.A. Rect. of St. *Peter-le-Poor, Lond.*

Rev. *John Starr*, Rector of *Stokeby Englifh, Devon.*

Rev. *Rob. Sutcliffe*, Curate of St. *Gregory's, Norwich.*

1795 Rev. *Wm. Sheepfhanks*, M.A. Prebendary of *Lincoln.*

Rev. *Edw. Scott*, M.A. Fellow of *Queen's* Coll. *Oxon.*

F. Stephens, Efq; Commiffioner of the Victualling-Board.

Rev. *J.S. Sawbridge*, M.A. *Stretton upon Dunfmore, Warw.*

Rev. *John Sandford*, LL B. Rector of *Cottefbrook, Northamp.*

Rev.

1796 Rev. *Ric. Slaney*, M.A. Vicar of *Penkridge, Staffordſh.*
John Sewell, LL.D. Doctors Commons.
Rev. *Tho. Wm. Shore*, M.A. Vicar of *Otterton, Devon.*
Rev. *Joſ. Atwell Small*, D.D. Prebendary of *Glocſter.* ·
Rev. *Thomas Scott*, M.A. Rector of *Little Oakley.*
Col. *Sibthorpe*, of the *South Lincoln* Militia.
1797 Rev. *Edw. Salter*, Rector of *Stratfeildſaye, Hants.*
Mr. *Thomas Sparks, Alderſgate-ſtreet.*
Rev. *Thelwall Saluſbury*, LL.B. Rector of *Gravely, Herts.*
Rev. *James Spirling*, Vicar of *Great Mapleſtead*, near
Halſtead, Eſſex.
Rev. *Thomas Slade*, M.A. Vicar of *Anſtrey, Warwickſh.*
C. S. *Strong*, Eſq; *Pancras Lane.-*
1798 Rev. *W. E. Sims,* B.A. *Fingringhoe, Eſſex.*
Rev. *Jonathan Stubbs*, Fellow of *New* College, *Oxford.*
Rev. *T. H. Spurrier*, LL.B. Vicar of *Layton, Eſſex.*
Rev. *Rich. Stopford*, Rector of *Barton, Northamptonſhire.*
Rev. *Thomas Salmon*, B.D. Rector of *Drymersfeild, Hants.*
John Sergent, Eſq; M.P. *Lavington*, near *Petworth, Suſſex.*
Rev. *John Skinner*, M.A. *Claverton*, near *Bath.*
Rev. *Humph. Sumner*, D.D. Provoſt of *King's* Coll. *Camb.*
1799 *Miller Southgate*, Eſq; *Guildford Street.*
Hon. and Rev. *Charles Stewart*, M.A. Fellow of *All
Souls* Coll. *Oxford.*
Rev. *Cha. Smith*, B.D. Miniſter of St. *Mary, Aldermanbury.*
Mr. *Thomas Simpkin*, of the *Strand.* ·

T.

1797 THE Moſt Noble the Marquis *Townſend, Rainham
Hall, Norfolk.*
1746 Rev. *Joſiah Tucker*, D.D. Dean of *Glocefter.*
Rev. *William Talbot*, M.A. Chancellor of *Sarum.*
1765 Rev. *Ferd.Travell*,M.A.Rector of*Upper Slaughter,Glocefl.*
John Toke, Eſq; *Godington* in *Kent.*

1767 Rev. *Hen. Hawkins Tremayne*, M.A. of *Heligan, Cornwall*.
1768 *Paul Turquand,* Efq; 73, *Houndfditch*.
1773 Mr. *Thomas Thurman, Devizes, Wilts*.
1774 Rev. —— *Thiftlethwaite, Sunning-Hill, Berks*.
1775 Rev. Sir *Harry Trelawny*, Bart. M.A. Prebendary of
     Exeter, and Vicar of *Eglofhayle, Cornwall*.
1776 Rev. *Tho. Taylor*, LL.D. Chaplain in Ord. to His Majefty.
     Rev. *Wm. Thomas*, M.A. Chanc. of the Church of *Llandaff*.
1782 Rev. *Ric. Twopeny*, M.A. Rector of *CaftertonParva, Rutl*.
1784 Rev. *Tho. Trevenen*, M.A. Rector of *Cardynham, Cornw*.
1786 Rev. *Jof. Turner*, D.D. Dean of *Norwich*.
     Rev. *Geo. S. Townley*, M.A. Rector of St. *Stephen's, Walbr*.
     Rev. *Edw. Townfhend*, M.A. Rector of *Henley upon Thames*.
1787 *Henry Thornton*, Efq; M. P. *Clapham*.
     Rev. *Francis Tutte*, M.A. Rector of *Shering, Effex*.
     Rev. *Edward Tew*, M.A. Fellow of *Eton* College.
     Edward Tomkinfon, Efq; *Boftock, Chefhire*.
     Rev. *Ja. Trebeck*, M.A. Rector of *Queenbithe, London*.
     Robert Thornton, Efq; M. P. *Clapham*.
1788 *Michael Angelo Taylor*, Efq; M. P. *Privy-Garden*.
     Rev. *Seth Thompfon*, M.A. Chaplain at *Kenfington* Palace.
     Rev. *Robert Thorpe*, Curate of *Buxton, Derbyfhire*.
     Wm. Tayleur, jun. Efq; *Buntingfdale, Salop*.
1789 Rev. *James Thom*, M.A. Rector of *Southacre, Norfolk*.
     Rev. *Wm. De Chair Tatterfall*, M. A. Vicar of *Wooton
     under Edge, Gloucefterfhire*.
     Rev. *Wm. Thomas*, B. A. Curate of *Goodneftone, Kent*.
     Rev. *Robert Thompfon*, LL.D. of *Kenfington*.
     Rev. *Chrift. Fred. Triebner*, of *Hull, Yorkfhire*.
1791 *Charles Townfhend*, Efq; *Old Burlington Street*.
     Francis Thwaites, Efq; *Bucklerfbury*.
     Rev. *Stephen Tucker*, Vicar of *Linftead, Kent*.
     Thomas Tipping, Efq; *Hardy Green*, near *Manchefter*.
1792 Rev. *Edw. Tatham*, D.D. Rector of *Lincoln* Coll. *Oxon*.
                                                      Rev.

1792 Rev. *Wm. Trickell,* M. A. Rector of *Charlton, Devon.*
1793 *Richard Tull,* Eſq; *Thatcham, Berks.*
Rev. *John Tatterſall,* M. A. Vicar of *Harwood* and
Ledſham, Yorkſhire.
Rev. *Tho. Thirlwall,* M. A. Lect. of St. *Dunſtan's, Stepney.*
1794 Rev. *Matt. Thomas, Sutton-Lodge, Surry.*
Rev. *W. J. Totton,* M. A. Rector of *Debden, Eſſex.*
Rev. *Moſes Toghill,* M. A. Prebendary of *Chicheſter.*
John Trevenen, Eſq; *Helſton, Cornwall.*
Rev. *Archer Thompſon,* M. A. Vicar of *Thatcham, Berks.*
Rev. *Fred. Tomkins,* M. A. Rector of *South Perrott, Dorſet*
Rev. *J. Thurlow,* LL.B. Vicar of *Gosſeild, Eſſex.*
1795 Rev. *Tho. Trevor Trevor,* LL. B. Prebendary of *Cheſter.*
1796 Rev. *T. Thwaites,* B.D. Rector of *Seagrave, Leiceſterſh.*
1797 Rev. *John Tucker,* Rector of *Graveſend, Kent.*
B. W. Trevelyan, Eſq; *Nether Witton,* near *Morpeth.*
Rev. *Walter Trevelyan,* M. A. Rector of St. *Mawgan*
and St. *Martin, Cornwall.*
John Tappenden, Eſq; *South Lambeth.*
1798 Rev. *Ric. Tillard,* M. A. Rector of *Bluntiſham, Hunts.*
Rev. *Jeremiah Triſt,* M. A. Vicar of *Veryan, Cornwall.*
Rev. *James Tomlin,* B. A. *Queen's* College, *Oxford.*
Colonel *Thornoon,* of the Firſt Regiment of Guards.
Rev. *William Tate,* M. A. Fellow of *Trinity* Coll. *Camb.*
1799 Rev. *Geo. A. Thomas,* M. A. Rector of *Woolwich, Kent.*
Arthur Tremayne, Eſq; *Sydenham, Devonſhire.*

V, U.

1798 R IGHT Hon. *Henry,* Earl of *Uxbridge.*
1776 Rev. *R. Uvedale,* D. D. Rector of *Langton, Lincolnſh.*
Rev. *William Vyſe,* LL.D. Archdeacon of *Coventry.*
1779 Rev. *William Vincent,* D.D. Sub-Almoner to His Majeſty.
Admiral *Vincent, Plymouth.*
1784 Rev. *Peter Vatas,* M.A. Miniſter of *Caverſham, Oxfordſh.*
Rev.

1786 Rev. *Benjamin Underwood*, M. A. Prebendary of *Ely*.
1788 Rev. *Dan. Veyſie*, B. D. Rector of *Plymtree*, *Devon*.
1789 *William Villers*, Eſq; *Birmingham*.
     Nicholas Vanſittart, Eſq; *Lincoln's-Inn*.
1791 *George Udney*, Eſq; *Calcutta*, *Bengal*.
1792 Rev. *Cha. Vincent*, M. A. of *Newbury*.
     Edward Vincent, Eſq; *South Mims*, *Middleſex*.
     Rev. *James Vickers*, M.A. Vicar of St. *Lawrence Jewry*.
     Rev. *John Chriſtian Chriſtopher Ubele*, Miniſter of a
     German Lutheran Congregation in *Spitalfields*.
     Rev. *Ric. Valpy*, D.D. Maſter of *Reading* School.
1793 Rev. *Edward Unwin*, M. A. *Pembroke* College, *Oxon*.
     Rev. *John Venn*, M. A. Rector of *Clapham*, *Surry*.
1796 Rev. *Edw. Vanſittart*, M. A. Rector of *Shotteſbrook*, *Berks*.
1797 Rev. *Wm. Van Mildert*, M. A. Rector of St. *Mary-le-Bow*.
     Rev. *Stonhouſe Vigor*, M. A. Rector of *Sunning-well*, near
     Abington.
1798 Rev. *Philip Vaillant*, M.A. *Ealing*, *Middleſex*.
1799 Rev. *Will. St. And. Vincent*, M.A. Student of *Ch.Ch.Oxford*.
     Rev. *Will.Vollans*, M.A. Rector of *Hemſworth*, near *Wakefield*.

W.

1787 H ON. and Right Rev. *Brownlow*, Lord Biſhop of
         Wincheſter.
1780 Right Rev. *Richard* Lord Biſhop of *Worceſter*.
1762 Right Hon. Lord *Willoughby de Broke*.
1795 Right Hon. *Horatio*, Lord *Walpole*, of *Woolterton*.
1763 Rev. *Rob. D. Waddilove*, M. A. Dean of *Ripon*.
     Rev. *Nathan Wetherell*, D. D. Dean of *Hereford*, and
     Maſter of *Univerſity* College, *Oxon*.
1764 Rev. *Charles Weſton*, M. A. Prebendary of *Durham*.
     Mr. *Joſeph Wells*, *Baſing Lane*.
     Rev. *Palmer Whalley*, M.A. Rector of *Ecton*, *Northamptonſh*.
1769 Rev. *H. Whitfeld*, D. D. Rector of St. *Margaret*, *Lothb*.
                                                        Rev.

1772 Rev. *J.Willoughby*, LL.B. *Hutton*, near *Tadcaster,Yorkfh.*
Samuel Wegg, Efq; *Hart-Street, Bloomfbury.*
.. ..Rev. *Edward Walls, Spilfby, Lincolnfhire.*
1773 Rev. *L. Wynne*, LL.D. *Queen Ann Street Weft, Cav. fq.*
Willoughby Wood, Efq; *Thorefby, Lincolnfhire.*
1774 Rev. *John Whitaker*, B. D. Rector of *Ruan Lanyhorne,*
near *Tregony, Cornwall.*
Rev. *James Geo.Warner*, M.A. Rector of *Milton, Berks.*
Rev. *Ric. Williams*, M.A. Vicar of *Horton Kirby, Kent.*
1775 *Samuel Waring*, Efq; *South-ftreet, Grofvenor-fquare.*
Rev. *Tho. Woodrooffe*, B.D. Rector of *Oakly, Surry.*
1777 *William Wilfon*, Efq; of the *Minories.*
1780 Rev. *Thomas Wintle*, B. D. Rector of *Brightwell, Berks.*
1781 Rev.*Ed.Whitmore*, M.A. Rector of *GreatHorwood,Bucks.*
Rev. *William Watkins*, Vicar of *Bucknell* in *Shropfhire.*
1782 Rev. *Tho. Wagftaffe*, M.A. Rector of *Barley, Herts.*
Rev. *John Weddred*, B.D. Vicar of St. *John Baptift*, Pe-
terborough, and Minor-Canon of the Cathedral.
1783 Rev.*Wm.Wrighte*, M.A. Clerk in Orders of St.*Martin's.*
Rev. *Tilly Walker*, M.A.Vicar of *MearsAfhby,Northamp.*
Rev. *R. Wharton*, M.A. Archdeacon of *Stow*, and
Rector of *Sigglefthorne, Yorkfh.*
1784 Rev. *Fra.Woodford*, M.A. Rector of *Anfford, Somerfetfh.*
Mr. *David Pike Watts*, of the *Minories, London.*
Rev. *Edward Wilfon*, D.D. Rector of *Afhurft*, in *Suffex.*
Richard Willding, Efq; *Llanrhaiad'r Hall, Denbighfhire.*
. Rev. *Edward Wilfon*, M.A. Canon of *Windfor.*
Rev. *Ric.Walton*, Rector of *Wootton*, in the *Ifle* of *Wight.*
1785 Rev. *Philip Woodhoufe, Hingham, Norfolk.*
1786 *John Watkins*, Efq; *Warrington, Lancafhire.*
William Wilberforce, Efq; M.P. *Weftminfter.*
Rev. *Henry Wilfon, Kirby-Caree, Norfolk.*
Rev. *Bafil Woodd*, M.A. Lecturer of St. *Peter's, Cornh.*
Lovelace Bigg Wither, Efq; *Manydown, Hants.*

Rev.

1786 Rev. *Ofborn Wighte*, M.A. Rector of *Ponfbury*, *Salop*.
Mr. *John Waring*, Barnes, *Surry*.
Rev. *Philip Webber*, M.A. Rector of *Mawnan*, *Cornwall*.
1787 Rev. *Stephen White*, LL.D Vicar of *Lenton* in *Linc*.
Rev. *Tho. W. Wrighte*, M.A. St. *Martin's in the Fields*.
Rev. *James Webfter*, LL.B. Archdeacon of *Gloucefter*.
John Wightwick, Efq; *Sandgates*, near *Chertfey*, *Surry*.
Rev. *John Wills*, D.D. Warden of *Wadham* Coll. *Oxford*.
Rev. *Walter Williams*, M.A. Vicar of *Harrow*, *Middx*.
Rev. *James Wilkinfon*, M.A. Prebendary of *Ripon*,
and Vicar of *Sheffield*, *Yorkfhire*.
Rev. *Ric. Waddington*, M.A. Rector of *Cavendifh*, *Suff*.
Rev. *E. W. Whitaker*, B.A. Rector of St. *Mildred's*,
and *All Saints*, *Canterbury*.
1788 Rev. *Robert Walker*, B.A. Vicar of St. *Winnow*, *Cornw*.
Rev. *Jofhua Wood*, M.A. Fellow of *Cath. Hall*, *Camb*.
Peter Waldo, Efq; *Mitcham* in *Surry*.
Rev. *John Wingfield*, D.D. Fellow of *Trin.* Coll. *Camb*.
1789 Rev. *John Williams*, *Yftradmeirig*, *Cardiganfhire*.
Rev. *Francis Willington*, Rector of *Walton upon Trent*.
Rev. *Jofeph White*, D.D. Prebendary of *Gloucefter*.
Rev. *Rob. Welton*, Vicar of *Sandridge*, *Herts*.
Rev. *John Williams*, M.A. *Llanrwft*, *Denbigh*.
Rev. *Wm. Wray*, Rector of *Darley*, in *Derbyfhire*.
Mr. *John Ward*, *Birmingham*.
Tho. W. Whalley, Efq; *Roche Court*, near *Fareham*, *Hants*.
Rev. *John Stanhawe Watts*, M.A. Rector of *Afhill*, *Norf*.
Henry Chriftopher Wife, Efq; *Priory*, *Warwick*.
Rev. *Wm. Whalley*, M.A. Rector of *Prefteign*, *Radnorfh*.
Rev. *Wm. Webb*, *Afhburn*, *Derbyfhire*.
Rev. *James Wood*, B.D. Fellow of St. *John's* Coll. *Camb*.
Wm. White, Efq; *Highbury Place*, *Middlefex*.
Rev. *Ja. Wood*, D.D. Rector of *Marfton Mortein*, *Beds*.
Rev. *Tho. Waddington*, M.A. Prebendary of *Ely*.
Rev.

1789 Rev. *Baldwin Wake*, Rector of *Riddlefworth, Norfolk.*
Rev. *John Waldron, Elmley, Worcefterfhire.*
Right Hon. Sir *W. Wynne*, LL.D. Dean of the Arches.
Rev. *Geo. Watts*, M. A. Vicar of *Uffington, Berks.*
1791 Rev. *David Williams, Heytefbury, Wilts.*
Rev. *Henry White*, Sacrift of *Litchfield* Cathedral.
Rev. *Thomas Wythe*, M. A. Vicar of *Eye, Suffolk.*
Rev. *Tho. D.Whitaker*, LL.B. *Holme*, near *Burnley,Lanc.*
Rev. *Cha. Wallington*, M. A. Rector of *Hackwell, Effex.*
Rev. *PeterWilliams*, Vicar of the Cath. Church of *Bangor.*
Nicholas Weftcomb, Efq; *Langford Grove, Effex.*
Rev. *Geo. Watfon*, D.D. Rector of *Rothbury, Northum.*
1792 Rev. *Wm. Ward*, Rector of *Myland, Colchefter.*
Rev. *James Walter*, B. A. *Brigg, Lincolnfhire.*
Rev. *Geo. Williams*, Lecturer of St. *Ann's, Limehoufe.*
Rev. *Wm. Williams*, M. A. Rector of *Bifhopfton, Wilts.*
1793 Mr. *Rob. Watkinfon, Manningtree, Effex.*
Tho. Windle, Efq; *Mile End Old Town, Middlefex.*
Rev. *John C.Woodhoufe, Donington,* near *Wolverhampton.*
Rev. *John Williams*, B.D. Rector of *Branfton, Northamp.*
1794 Rev. *John Woolcombe*, M.A. *Briton-Side, Plymouth.*
Rev. *Rob. Walker*, Rector of *Shingham, Norfolk.*
Rowland Williams, Efq; *Beaumaris, Anglefea.*
Rev. *EllisWynne*, B.A. Curate of *Foclas* Chapel, *Denbigh.*
Rev. *Tho. Willis*, LL. D. Rector of St. *George's, Bloomfb.*
Sir *Jacob Wolf*, Bart. *Mellyfont Abbey*, near *Wells.*
Rev. *Peter Williams*, B. A. Rector of *Lanrug* and
Llanberris, Carnarvonfhire.
Rev. *Fra. Hyde Wollafton*, M.A.Vicar of *South Weald, Effex.*
Rev. *Edw. Walfby*, D.D. Prebendary of *Canterbury.*
Rev. *David Williams*, Rector of *Selworthy, Somerfetfhire.*
Mr. *Thomas Wilkes, Blockley, Worcefterfhire.*
1795 Rev. *E.Williams*, Minifter of *Uffington* and *Battlefeild,Salop.*

L   Rev.

1795 Rev. *John Wilgreſs*, D.D. *Eltham, Kent.*
Rev.*Wm.Farley Wilkinſon*,M.A. Rect. of *Needham, Norf.*.
Rev. *Henry John Wollaſton*, M.A. Chaplain in Ordinary
to his Majeſty.
Rev. *Rob. Wetherell*, LL.B. Fellow of *New* Coll. *Oxon.*.
Rev. *Sam. Wix*, B.A. of *Chriſt* Coll. *Camb.* .
Rev. *Ph.Wroughton*, M.A. Vicar of *Shabbington,Bucks.*
1796 Mr. *William Wilſon*, *Milk-ſtreet, London.*
Mr. *Joſhua Watſon*, *Mincing-lane, London*.
Rev. *Dawſon Warren*, B.A. Vicar of *Edmonton, Midd.*.
Samuel Waring, Jun. Eſq; of the *Temple.*
Rev. *John Whitmore,*. M.A. Rector of *Polſtead, Suffolk.*
Rev.*R.Webſter*, B.D. Rector of *Aſton-le-Wall,Northam.*
Rev. *T. Wright*, M.A. Rector of St. *Mary,.Whitechapel.*
Rev.*Tho.Williams*, M.A. Vicar of *Langadock, Carmarth.*
1797 Rev. *John Wooll*, M.A. Curate of *Eaſton, Hants.*
James Woodbridge, Eſq; *James-ſtreet, Bedford-row.*
Rev. *William Whitelock*, M.A. *Soho-ſquare.*
Hon. *Charles Godfrey*, Baron *Wolf*, LL.D. *London.*
Rev. *R. C. Whalley*, Rector of *Horſington, Somerſet.*
Rev. *Edward Ward*, B.A. Chaplain in the Royal Navy..
1798 Rev. *Godfrey Woolley*, M.A. Vicar of *Hutton. Buchell,*
Yorkſhire.
Rev. *John Williams*, B.A. of St. *Mary's Hall, Oxford.*
Rev. *John James Watſon*, M.A. Vicar of *Hackney, Midd.*
Rev. *John Williams*, M.A. Rector of *Merſton Magna,*
and *Aſhington, Somerſet.*
Rev. *W.B. Whitfeld*, M.A. Fellow of St. *John's* Coll.
Cambridge.
Rev. *Francis Wrangham*, M.A. of *Trinity* Coll. *Camb.*
Mr. *George Walker, Mancheſter.*
R. W. Wynne, Eſq; *Garthewin, Denbighſhire.*
Hon. and Rev. *Gerard Weſley*, Chaplain in Ordinary to
his Majeſty.

Rev..

1798 Rev. *John Whitaker*, LL. B. Rector of *Garforth*, near *Leeds*.
Rev. *William Wyatt*, M. A. Rector of *Framlingham*, *Suffolk*.
Robert Williams, Efq; Alderman of *London*.
Rev. *William Shippen Willes*, M.A. Minifter of *Cirencefter*.
Rev. *Geo.Whitmore*, B.D.Sen. Fellow of St. *John's* Coll. *Camb*.
Rev. *Tho. Woodcock*, M.A. Rector of *Swellington*, near *Leeds*.
Rev. *Tho. Whateley*, Vicar of *Cookham*, *Berks*.
1799 *William Wickham*, Efq; M.P. one of the under Secre-
taries of State.
Rev. *Hen. Whytehead*, B.A. *Hornfea*, *Eaft Riding of York*.
Rev. *Tho. Whipham*, M.A. *Woking*, near *Ripley*, *Surry*.
Rev. *Tho. H. Wayett*, D. D. Vicar of *Pinchbeck*, *Spalding*.
Rev. *Robert Woodbridge*, Curate of *Hedgerley*, *Bucks*.
Rev. *T. W. Weftern*, M. A. Rector of *Rivenhall*, *Effex*.
Rev. *Geo.Wells*, Rector of *Wefton*, in the Diocefe of *Chichefter*.
Rev. *John Laycock Wetherell*, Rector of *Rufhton*, *Nor-
thamptonfhire*.
William Wix, Efq; *Iflington*, *Middlefex*.
Rev. *Henry Wife*, M.A. Rector of *Charlewood*, *Surry*.

Y.

1766 THE Moft Rev. *William*, Lord Archbifhop of *York*.
1785 Rev. *Duke Yonge*, M.A. Vicar of *Cornwood*, *Devon*.
1787 Rev. *John Young*, LL.B. *Clapton*.
1794 Mr. *Simon Andrews Younge*, Merchant, *Sheffield*.
Rev. *Philip Yorke*, M.A. Prebendary of *Ely*.
1798 Rev. *Richard Yates*, Chaplain of *Chelfea* College.

Z.

1780 REV. *Thomas Zouch*, M. A. Rector of *Scrayingham*,
Yorkfhire.

N. B. *Errata* in this Catalogue, if communicated to the
Secretary, will be corrected.

FOREIGN MEMBERS.

1762 **R**EV. *James Renaud Boullier*, Minifter of the *French* Church at *Amfterdam*.

1764 Rev. *John Auguft. Urlfperger*, D. D. Senior of the Miniftry at *Augfpurg*.

1774 Rev. *Chriftian Lewis Gerling*, D.D. Senior of the Miniftry at *Hamburgh*.

1779 Rev. *Aaron Mathefius*, M. A. *Sweden*.

L A D I E S, Annual Subfcribers.

1795 Her Royal Highnefs,. the PRINCESS OF WALES.

A.

1797 **R**IGHT Hon. Lady *Louifa*, Countefs of *Aylesford.*
1773 **R** Mrs. *Afhby*, *Haflebeech*, *Northamptonfhire*.
Mrs. *Alnutt*.
1781 Mrs. *Allanfon*, *Grofvenor-Square*.
1790 Mrs. *Maria Arden*, *Stockport*, *Chefhire*.
1795 Mrs. *Allan*, *Mill Green Houfe*, *Ingateftone*.
1796 Mrs. *A. E. Ayliffe*, of *Surbiton Lodge*, near *Kingfton*.
Mrs. *Adderley*, *Hams*, *Warwickfhire*.
1798 Mrs. *Margaret Eliz. Arden*, *Longcrofts*, *Staffordfhire*.
1799 Mifs *Frances Afhburnham*, *Great George-ftr. Hanover-fq*.
Mrs. *Rebecca Afheton*, *Beaconsfield*, *Bucks*.
Mrs. *Lydia Amphlett*, *Gower-ftreet*.

Mrs,

6

Time of
Admiffion.   [85]

1799 Mrs. *M. Auftin, Kippingfton*, near *Seven Oaks, Kent.*
Mrs. *Rob. Adeane, Walton*, near *Saffron Walden, Effex.*

B.

1797 MOST Noble the Marchionefs of *Bath.*
1779 Right Hon. Countefs of *Bute.*
1769 Mrs. *Banks, Chelfea.*
Mifs *Banks, ditto.*
1783 Mifs *Barnfton, Bath.*
Hon. Mrs. *Bofcawen*, of *South-Audley-Street.*
1784 Mrs. *Peploe Birch, Garnftone, Herefordfhire.*
1787 Mrs. *Elizabeth Bagott.*
Mrs. *Bertie, Devonfhire-place.*
1788 Mrs. *Margaret Balwin, Plaxtoole, Kent.*
Lady *Bridges, Goodnefton, Kent.*
1790 Mrs. *E. Buckle, Upper Seymour-ftreet.*
Mrs. *Mary Bunney, Bath.*
1791 Mrs. *Jane Butts, Geftingthorpe, Effex.*
Mrs. *D'Arcy Boulton.*
Mrs. *Blackwell, North Cerney, Gloucefterfhire.*
Lady *Banks, Soho-fquare.*
1792 Mifs *Bourne, Afhford, Kent.*
Mrs. *Sarah Beachcroft, Bloomfbury-place.*
1793 Mrs. *Mary Bowles, Northafton, Oxfordfh.*
1794 Mifs *Brunette, Beverley, Yorkfhire.*
Mrs. *Bolton, Nottingham.*
1795 Mrs. *Mary Bateman, Guilfborough, Northamptonfhire.*
1797 Mrs. *Mary Browne, Tullantire Hall, Cumberland.*
Hon. Mrs. *Barrington, Cavendifh-fquare.*

C.

1771 RIGHT Hon. Lady *Cremorne, Stanhope-ftreet.*
1787 Right Hon. the Countefs Dowager of *Chatham.*
1789 Right Hon. the Countefs of *Chatham.*

Right

1794 Right Hon. Lady *Louifa Clayton.*
1761 Mrs. *Elizabeth Coote, Rotherbithe.*
1762 Mrs. *Cornwall, Chart Park, Surry.*
1772 Mrs. *Gilbert Cooper, Thurgaton, Nottinghamſhire.*
1783 Lady *Cave, Upper Groſvenor-ſtreet.*
     Mrs. *Martha Cranmer, Nurſling, Hants.*
1785 Mrs. *Charlton, Ludford,* near *Ludlow.*
     Miſs *Cave, New Norfolk-Street.*
1787 Mrs. *Maria Cowper, Cole Green, Hartingfordbury.*
     Miſs *Creuze, Beddington, Surry.*
1790 Mrs. *A. Chamberlaine, Charlton, Kent.*
1792 Miſs *Clarke,* of *Tooting, Surry.*
     Mrs. *Harriot Cowper, Overlegh, Cheſter.*
     Lady *Chambers, Somerſet Houſe, London.*
1797 Mrs. *Coke,* of *Holkham.*
     Hon. Mrs. *Cadogan, Wallingford, Berks.*
1798 Mrs. *Jane Cotton, Rugeley, Staffordſhire.*
1799 Mrs. *Frances Clarke, Ruſlip, Middleſex.*
     Mrs. *Mary Carter, Canterbury.*

D.

1791   HER Grace the Ducheſs of *Devonſhire.*
1788   Rt. Hon. Lady *Dundas, Arlington-ſtreet, Piccadilly.*
1794 Rt. Hon. Counteſs Dowager of *Darley, Hereford-ſtreet.*
     Rt. Hon. Counteſs of *Darnley, Cobham Hall, Rocheſter.*
1774 Mrs. *Diana Daſhwood, Stanford-Hall, Notts.*
     Mrs. *Ann Daſhwood, Well-Hall, Lincolnſhire.*
1776 Mrs. *Daubeny, North Bradley, Wiltſhire.*
     Mrs. *Dicey, Claybrook, Leiceſterſhire.*
     Mrs. *De Luc.*
1779 Mrs. *Douglas, St. Alban's,* near *Wingham, Kent.*
1785 Mrs. *Denward, Hardres Court, Kent.*
1786 Mrs. *Tyrwhitt Drake, Shardeloes, Bucks.*

Mrs.

1787 Mrs. *Docton, Plymouth.*
1788 Mrs. *Denison, Gay-street, Bath.*
1790 Mrs. *Elizabeth Dalton, Stanmore,* in *Middlesex.*
     Mrs. *Elizabeth Dutens, Leicester-square.*
     Mrs. *Duppa, Hackney.*
1796 Mrs. *Diana Dowdeswell, Grosvenor-place.*
1797 Mifs *Magdalen Daubuz, Truro, Cornwall.*

E.

1773 M R S. *Eeles, Great Cumberland-street.*
1782 M Mrs. *Elizabeth Ella, Newark, Nottinghamshire.*
1786 Mifs *Edmunds, Worsbrough, Yorkshire.*
1797 Mrs. *Enfor, Bath.*
     Mrs. *A. Ewbank, Londerbro', Yorkshire.*

F.

1791 R IGHT Hon. Countefs of *Fortefcue.*
1793 R Right Hon. Lady *Forrefter, Bedgebury, Kent.*
1766 Mrs. *Judith Finch, Cavendish-square.*
1793 Mifs *Fifher, Warwick.*
1797 Mifs *Margaret Frank, Campfal,* near *Doncafter.*
1798 Mifs *Ann Finch, Goodneftone, Kent.*
     Mrs. *Jane Floyer, Stafford,* near *Dorchefter, Dorfet.*
1799 Mrs. *Eliz. Fleming, Stoneham Park,* near *Southampton.*

G.

1786 R IGHT Hon. Lady *Gallway, Hill-ftreet.*
1770 R Mrs. *Gold, Loughborough.*
1772 Mrs. *Ann Gwatkin, Bath.*
1778 Mrs. *Garnier, Wickham, Hants.*
     Hon. Mrs. *Grant, Hill-ftreet, Berkeley-square.*
1791 Mrs. *Gray, York.*
     Mrs. *Elizabeth Gough, Bryanftone-ftreet.*
1792 Lady *Grantham, Whitehall.*

Mrs.

1792 Mrs. *E. G. Gregory, Park-ftreet, Grofvernor-fquare.*
1793 Lady *Graham, Whitwell,* near *York.*
1794 Mrs. *Eliz. Gofling, Lincoln's-inn-fields.*
1795 Lady *Cath. Graham, Netherby, Cumberland.*
1797 Hon. Mifs *Charlotte Grimftone, Gorambury, St. Alban's.*
     Mrs. *Gally,* Great *Ruffel-ftreet.*
1798 Mrs. *Mary Gratwicke, Danny, Suffex.*
1799 Mrs. *Eliz. Gipps, Harbledown,* near *Canterbury.*

H.

1790 **R**IGHT Hon. the Countefs of *Harcourt.*
1795   Right Hon. Vifcountefs Dowager *Hereford, Stan-*
      way, Glocefterfhire.
1798 Right Hon. Lady *Elizabeth Finch Hatton.*
1766 Mifs *Harvey, Hinxworth, Herts.*
1774 Lady *Herries, St. James's-ftreet.*
1779 Mrs. *Hacket, Moxhull, Warwickfhire.*
1783 Mrs. *Hatt, Faringdon, Berks.*
    Mifs *Huffey, Afhford, Kent.*
1784 Mrs. *Humphreys, Claremount-hill, Salop.*
1787 Mrs. *Mary Hervey, Canterbury.*
    Mrs. *Mary Hooper,* Town-hall, *Worcefter.*
1788 Mrs. *Hopkins, Windfor.*
1790 Mrs. *Hutchings, Dittifham,* in *Devon.*
    Mrs. *Ann Holbeach, Farnborough, Warwickfhire.*
1791 Mifs *Hannah How, Plymouth.*
1792 Mrs. *Sarah Haws, Great Marlow, Bucks.*
    Mifs *Eliz. Gerring Harrifon.*
1793 Mrs. *Felicia Horne, Uxbridge.*
    Mrs. *Sarah Horfeley, Sawbridgworth, Herts.*
    Mrs. *Higginfon, Harley-ftreet.*
1795 Mrs. *Sarah Heathfield, Croydon, Surry.*
    Mrs. *Harris, Hayne, Devonfhire.*
    Mrs. *Hayward, Canterbury.*

                                     Mrs.

1796 Mrs. *Ann Hale*, *Ingsdon*, *Devon*.
　　　 Mifs *Charlotte Huffey*, *Afhford*, *Kent*.
1798 Mrs. *Sarah Hayter*, of the *Clofe*, *Salifbury*.
　　　 Mrs. *Hocker*, *Wefton*, near *Bath*.
1799 Mrs. *Hon. Huddleftone*, *Down Place*, near *Windfor*.
　　　 Mifs *Hadfley*, *Ware Priory*, *Herts*.
　　　 Mifs *M. Hadfley*, *Ditto*.

I.

1787 **R**IGHT Hon. Lady *St. John*.
1776 　 Mrs. *Ireland*, *Newark upon Trent*, *Notts*.
1789 Mrs. *Iremonger*, *Wherwell*, *Hants*.
1790 Mrs. *Elizabeth Jennings*, *Harlington*, *Bedfordfhire*.
1791 Mrs. *Johnfon*, *Burleigh-fields*, *Leicefterfhire*.
1792 Lady *Jones*, *Cavendifh-fqare*.
1794 Mrs. *Jane Johnes*, *Stafod*, *Cardiganfhire*.

K.

1799 **R**IGHT Hon. Lady *Kingfton*, *Stratford Place*.
1777 　 Mrs. *Knightley*, *Grofvenor-Square*.
1782 Mifs *Kerridge*, *Whitton White Houfe*, near *Ipfwich*.
1788 Mifs *Keene*, *Charles Street*, *Berkeley Square*.
1789 Mrs. *Eliz. Knightley*, *Prefton*, near *Daventry*.
1795 Mrs. *Judith Kingfbury*, *Caiftor*, near *Yarmouth*.
1799 Mrs. *Kempftone*, *Helftone*, *Cornwall*.

L.

1792 **R**IGHT Hon. *Anne*, Baronefs *Lyttelton*.
1794 　 Right Hon. Lady *Lucas*, St. *James's Square*.
1783 Mrs. *Lawes*, *Brighton*.
　　　 Mrs. *Legard*, *Etton*, *Yorkfhire*.
　　　 Mrs. *E. Lightbody*, *Liverpool*.
1784 Mrs. *Lonfdale*, *Badburham*, *Cambridgefhire*.
1788 Hon. Mrs. *Leigh*, *Stoneleigh Abbey*, *Warwickfhire*.
　　　　　　　M　　　　　　　　　　　Mrs.

1790 Mrs. *Lambe, Mountsfield, Rye, Suffex.*
Lady *Lloyd.*
1792 Mrs. *Lamplugh, Knarefborough, Yorkfhire.*
1794 Mrs. *Eliz. Lechmere, Hanlay Caftle, Worcefterfhire.*
1797 Mrs. *Long, Lincoln's-inn-fields.*
1799 Lady *Catherine Long, Draycot, Wilts.*
Mrs. *E. S. Lawrence, Canterbury.*
Mrs. *M. Lightbody, Birchfeild, Liverpool.*

M.

1788 RIGHT Hon. Countefs Dowager of *Mansfield.*
1797 Right Hon. Lady *Robert Manners, Grofvenor-fquare.*
1798 Right Hon. Lady Vicountefs *Myddleton.*
1781 Lady *Mordaunt, Walton, Warwickfhire.*
Lady *Mill, Arlingham Court, Gloucefterfhire.*
Mrs. *Jane Marriott, Perfhore, Worcefterfhire.*
1790 Mrs. *Hannah More,* the *Adelphi, London.*
1791 Lady *Catharine Murray, Guildford-ftreet.*
Mrs. *Mafter,* of the *Abbey, Cirencefter, Gloucefterfhire.*
1793 Mrs. *M'Culloh, Lincoln's-inn-fields.*
Mrs. *Mills, Portman-Square, London.*
1794 Mrs. *Dorothy Monck.*
1795 Mrs. *Moore, Helftone, Cornwall.*
1796 Mifs *Milles, Queen-ftreet, May Fair.*
Mrs. *Mytton,* of *Lythewood,* near *Shrewfbury.*
Mifs *Anne Mackilwain, Lymington.*
1797 Mrs. *Ifabella Market, Luddefdown,* near *Rochefter.*
Mrs. *Mary May, Bedford-fquare.*
1798 Hon. Mrs. *Marfham, Boxley, Kent.*
1799 Mrs. *Eliz. Murray, Rapley,* near *Abresford.*

9

Mrs.

N.

1776 **M** R S. *Neville, Willingore, Lincolnfhire.*
1793 Mrs. *Cath. Nicholfon, Liverpool.*
1794 Mrs. *Sibella Neufville, Lymington, Hants.*
1796 Mrs. *Diana Nowell, Cavendifh. Square.*

O.

1798 Right Hon. Lady *H. Ofborne, Chickfand's Priory, Bedfd.*

P.

1775 **R** IGHT Hon. Lady *Pelham, Stratton-ftreet.*
1786 Right Hon. Countefs *Paulet.*
1798 Right Hon. Lady *Maria Price.*
1772 Mrs. *Porter, No. 24, Gower-ftreet.*
1785 Mrs. *Catherine Pennant.*
1788 Mifs *Pares, Leicefter.*
Mrs. *Anna Palmer, Bifrons, Wanftead, Effex.*
1790 Mrs. *Margaret Penrofe, Carwethenack, Cornwall.*
1793 Mrs. *Mary Parry,* of *Ruabone, Denbighfhire.*
1797 Mrs. *Elizabeth Peers, Leftwithiel, Cornwall.*
Mifs *Frances Dorothy Pender, Treliffick, Cornwall.*
1798 Hon. Mrs. *Pole, Hanover-fquare.*
Mrs. *Mary Judith Paulett, Hingham, Norfolk.*
Mrs. *Sufan March Phillips, More Critchill, Dorfet.*
Mrs. *Puget, John-ftreet, Bedford-row.*
Lady *Parkyns, Bunny Park, Notts.*

Q.

1793 Mrs. *Quicke, Paragon Buildings, Bath.*

R.

1771 **R** IGHT Hon. Countefs of *Rothes.*
1786 Right Hon. Lady *Rolle.*
M 2   Mrs.

1753 Mrs. *Raitt, Huntingdon:*
1772 Mrs. *Rogers, Berkely, Somerſetſhire.*
1783 Mrs. *Arabella Rawdon, Cheſter.*
      Mrs. *Ravenhill, Bath.*
1788 Dowager Lady *Rogers,, Plymouth.*
      Mrs. *Reed, Hackney.*
1797 Lady *Rooke.*
1798 Mrs. *Marianne Rooke, Lymington, Hants.*
      Mrs. *Ridſdale, Widow, Leeds, Yorſhire.*

S.

1796 HER Grace the Duchefs of *Somerſet.*
1775   Right Hon. Countefs Dowager *Spencer.*
1791 Right Hon. Lady *Sherborne, Sherborne, Glouceſterſh.*
1793 Moſt Hon. the Marchionefs of *Stafford.*
1787 Right Hon. Lady *Sondes, Groſvenor-ſquare.*
1771 Mrs. *Seale, St. Sidwell's, Exeter.*
1785 Mrs. *Mary Spooner, Olton-Houſe,* near *Birmingham.*
      Mrs. *Snow, Clipſham, Rutlandſhire.*
1789 Mrs. *Anna Maria Shipley, Twyford,* near *Wincheſter.*
1790 Mrs. *B. Spooner, Elmdon-Houſe,* near *Birmingham.*
1791 Mrs. *Charlotte Selwyn, Bath.*
      Mifs *M. S. Saltonſtall, Hillingdon, Middleſex.*
1794 Mrs. *Ann Papwell Smith, Bredon, Worceſterſhire.*
      Mifs *M. Smith, Hillingdon, Middleſex.*
      Mifs *Sheppard, Denham, Bucks.*
1796 Mrs. *Saltmarche, Saltmarche,* near *Howden, Yorkſhire.*
1797 Lady *Stapleton, Gray's Court,* near *Henley, Oxon.*
1799 Mrs. *Rebecca Simſon, Red Lion-ſquare.*
      Mrs. *Starkie, Royſton,* near *Mancheſter.*
      Mrs. *Strachan, Lower Tooting.*

Mrs.

T.

1772 **MRS.** *Tomlinfon, Somerfet Street.*
1783 **M** Lady *Twyfden, Jennings, Kent.*
1787 Mrs. *Trimmer, Brentford.*
1788 Hon. Mrs. *Talbot, Barton, Gloucefterfhire.*
     Mrs. *Twigge, Derby.*
1794 Mrs. *Tighe, Clanville Lodge,* near *Andover, Hants.*
1795 Mrs. *F. M. A. Totton, Debden, Effex.*
     Mifs *Mary Tucker, Sealyham,* near *Haverford Weft.*
1796 Mifs. *Mary Dorothy Torkington, Worcefter.*
1799 Mrs. *Thompfon, Kirby Hall,* near *Boroughbridge, Yorkfh.*
     Mrs. *Charlotte Thompfon, Waverley Abbey,* near *Farnham.*
     Mrs. *Frances Sarah Thomas, Woolwich, Kent.*

V.

1790 **R** IGHT Hon. the Countefs of *Uxbridge.*
1789 **R** Mrs. *Vanfittart, Blackheath.*
1790 Mrs. *Elizabeth Unwin, Mansfield, Notts.*
1798 Mrs. *Udney, Teddington, Middlefex.*
     Mifs *Vanfittart, Blackheath.*
     Hon. Mrs. Geo. *Villers, Upper Grofvenor-ftreee.*

W.

1791 **R** Ight Hon. Countefs of *Waldegrave, Naveftock, Effex.*
1764 **R** Mrs. *Watfon, New Norfolk-ftreet.*
1776 Mrs. *Wood.*
1782 Mrs. *Whetham, Kirklington, Notts.*
1787 Lady *Wilfon, Charlton, Kent.*
     Mrs. *Waller, Chefterton Hall,* near *Stilton.*
     Mrs. *Wordfworth, Wadfworth, Yorkfhire.*
     Mrs. *Warsfold, Edmonton.*
1778 Mrs. *Waldo, Mitcham, Surry.*
     Lady *Wake, Courteen Hall, Northamptonfhire.*

                                        Mrs.

1788 Mrs. *Warton*, of *Winchſter*.
  Mrs. *Ann Wood, Devonſhire Place*.
1790 Mrs. *Pere Williams, Hoddeſdon, Herts*.
1791 Miſs *Whitbread, Portman-ſquare*.
1792 Mrs. *Williams, Nethway-houſe, Devon*.
  Mrs. *Suſanna Walker, Woodſtock, Oxon*.
  Mrs. *Iſabella Wyatt, Weſt Grinſted, near Horſham, Suſſex*.
1795 Mrs. *Anne White, Lower Brook-ſtreet*.
  Mrs. *Suſanna Whatman, Vinters, near Maidſtone*.
  Mrs. *Ann Weſtmoreland, Billingborough, Lincolnſhire*.
  Mrs. *Ann Whitaker, Loughton-Houſe, Eſſex*.
1798 Miſs *Wix, Iſlington, Middleſex*.
  Miſs *Ann White, Chillington, near Blandford*.
  Mrs. *Jane Worthington, Upper Tooting, Surry*.

Y.

1793 Miſs *Portia Young, Abbey Houſe, Chertſey*.
  Mrs. *Yarborough, Campſmount, Doncaſter*.

N. B. Ladies ballotted on the *Liſt of Annual Subſcribers*, are furniſhed with Books, on the Terms of the Society.

Nº II.

THAT the CHARITY SCHOOLS might answer the true Purpose for which they were
erected, the Society have, in their *Circular
Letters* to their Correspondents, recommended that,
with their Inftructions in Religion and Piety, they
fhould join all proper Methods of inuring the Children to *Labour* and *Induſtry* ; and in their Circular
Letter *A. D.* 1712, they have thefe Words:

"AND becaufe fome have apprehended, that the
" placing fo many of them out Apprentices to Ma-
" nual Trades, as is now generally done, may oc-
" cafion, in Time, a Want of Servants, efpecially
" in Hufbandry ; the Society recommend it to your
" Confideration, whether the bringing up the Chil-
" dren to Hufbandry, or putting them out to Ser-
" vices, at Sea, or in fober Families, may not be
" more ufeful to the Publick, and no lefs beneficial
" to themfelves."

IN the Year 1719, they recommended the fame
Thing to their Correfpondents, in the following
Words :

"NEXT to improving the Minds of the Poor
" in all neceffary Chriftian Knowledge, the Society
" have defired, and do again earneftly intreat all
" their Correfpondents, to ufe their utmoft Endea-
" vours to get fome Kind of Labour added to the
" Inftruction given to Children in the Charity
" Schools;

Circular
Letter.
1712.

1719.

" Schools; as *Husbandry* in any of its Branches,
" *Spinning, Sewing, Knitting*, or any other useful
" Employment; to which the particular Manufac-
" tures of their respective Countries may lead them.
" This will bring them to an Habit of Industry, as
" well as prepare them for the Business by which
" they are afterwards to subsist in the World, and
" effectually obviate an Objection against the Cha-
" rity Schools, that they tend to take poor Children
" off from those servile Offices which are necessary
" in all Communities, and for which the wise Go-
" vernor of the World has by his Providence de-
" signed them."

Circular
Letter.
1720. " THE best Means of employing the Poor has
" always had a Share in the Thoughts of the wisest
" Men in this Kingdom; and the present State of
" Affairs, with respect to our Trade, seems to re-
" quire a Continuance of your Care and Applica-
" tion, to promote those Employments among the
" Children educated in Charity Schools, which may
" be most for the Service of the Publick; so that
" beside *Reading, Writing*, and *Arithmetick*, and in-
" structing them in the Principles and Rules of our
" holy Religion, they ought also to be inured to some
" sort of profitable *Labour* or *Business*.
   " IT has been observed by a worthy Correspond-
" ing Member, that where, in the Want of other
" Labour, the Children in the Country go a Mile
" or two to School, even that has contributed to
" make them robust and active; and that *Garden-*
" *ing, Plowing, Harrowing*, or other servile Labour
" every other Day for their Parents, has been no
" Prejudice to their Progress in Learning."

" IT

[97]

" It is not eafy to prefcribe fuch an Employ as
" would fuit all Parts of the Kingdom; and there-
" fore it muft be left to the Prudence of thofe who
" are intrufted with the Management of Charity
" Schools, to chufe fuch Employments for the Chil-
" dren, as they fhall judge to be moft practicable in
" their refpective Places; and if any in your Neigh-
" bourhood have been fo happy as to fall into a pro-
" per Method for employing poor Children, you are
" defired to fignify it in as particular a Manner as you
" can ; that when the Society are furnifhed with a
" greater Variety of fuch Methods, they may be com-
" municated to the Publick for general Practice."

(margin: Circular Letter 1722.)

" And though the Manner of employing the Poor
" may, at firft, be attended with fome Difficulty, by
" reafon of the Variety of Manufactures in the King-
" dom, and the Materials neceffary for them, which
" all Places do not equally afford ; yet wherever an
" Attempt has been made (though by Means perhaps
" at firft not appearing very probable) it has feldom
" failed of producing fome good Effect : for not-
" withftanding the Produce of the Manufactures,
" wherein the Poor are employed, fhould happen
" to be but fmall, yet if they are kept from Idlenefs
" and Beggary, and inured to a fober and induftrious
" Way of Living, the good Effects thereof, as
" well to themfelves as to the Publick, will fully
" compenfate all the Pains that fhall be taken
" therein."

(margin: Circular Letter 1725.)

" The general Ufefulnefs of *Hufbandry* to this
" Nation, the real Want there has been of Perfons
" to be employed in it, and the Mortality that has
" lately happened in many Counties, efpecially

(margin: Circular Letter 1729.)

N   " among

" among the lower and more laborious Sort of
" People, are, in the Opinion of the Society, all of
" them, very good Reasons to engage their Mem-
" bers to use their utmoft Endeavours that poor
" Children may be bound out *Apprentices* to that
" Bufinefs; which would filence one of the moft
" popular Clamours that has been raifed againft
" Charity Schools. This Concern therefore, which
" fo nearly affects the common Intereft of our Coun-
" try, is particularly recommended by the Society to
" all their Members."

FROM thefe *Extracts* it will appear, how care-
ful this Society has always been to obviate the common Objections made againft the Charity Schools,
that they only breed up Children in Idlenefs and
Pride: And it muft not be omitted, that as early as
the Year 1712, they particularly recommended,
" That however thefe Children are difpofed of, it
" will be very neceffary before-hand to teach them
" that great Leffon of *true Humility*, which our
" Saviour has prefcribed to all that will be his Dif-
" ciples; left the Advantages they receive from a
" pious Education, fhould incline them to put too
" great a Value upon themfelves; and therefore
" that the Mafters be often put in Mind of guard-
" ing the Children under their Care, as much as
" poffible, againft fuch dangerous Conceits; and in
" order thereunto, to inftruct them very carefully in
" the Duties of Servants, and Submiffion to Supe-
" riors."

AND knowing that it is of the higheft Importance to the Welfare of the Charity Schools, to remove all Occafion of Complaint againft them as
Nurferies of *Difaffection* to the Government, They

acquainted

acquainted their Members in Town and Country,
" That his Grace the Archbifhop of *Canterbury*
" having heard fome Complaints againft the Con-
" duct of certain Teachers in thefe Schools, on this
" Head, did, in 1716, write a Letter to the Truftees
" of the Schools in and about *London,* earneftly ex-
" horting them *rigoroufly to animadvert upon all,*
" *whether Children or Teachers, who either appear,*
" *or fuffer them to appear at any Time in publick,*
" *to affront the Government, and bear a Part in thofe*
" *Tumults and Riots, which are fo great a Scandal,*
" *as well as Prejudice, to the good Order and Peace*
" *of the Realm. And likewife, if there be any Ca-*
" *techifms or Inftitutions taught in any of thefe*
" *Schools, that meddle with political or party Princi-*
" *ples, that they ought immediately to be thrown afide,*
" *as pernicious to the original Defign of thefe pious*
" *Nurferies.*"

So me Time after this, his Grace, in a particular
Manner, recommended it to the Truftees of the
Charity Schools in and about *London*; " To require
" all the Mafters and Miftreffes under their Di-
" rection, not only to take the Oaths to the Go-
" vernment before their Admiffion, but at the
" Time of their Admiffion to fubfcribe to fome fuch
" folemn Promife, or Declaration, as the following,
" *viz. That they do heartily acknowledge his Majefty*
" *King GEORGE, to be the only lawful and*
" *rightful King of thefe Realms; and will to the*
" *utmoft of their Power educate the Children com-*
" *mitted to their Charge, in a true Senfe of their*
" *Duty to him as fuch: That they will not, by any*
" *Words or Actions, do any thing whereby to leffen*
" *their Efteem of, or their Obedience to the prefent*
N 2   " *Govern-*

" *Government: That upon all publick Days, when*
" *their Children may be likely to appear among any*
" *diforderly Perfons, they will do their beft to keep them*
" *in, and feverely punifh them, if they fhall bear of*
" *their running into any Tumults, cr publick Meet-*
" *ings, contrary to the good Order of fuch Schools and*
" *Scholars."*

SEVERAL other Prelates have earneftly preffed
the like Exhortations, in their Sermons at the Anniverfary Meetings of the Charity Schools, as well as
on other Occafions; and the Society think it incum-
bent on them to ufe all their Intereft to procure a
general Conformity to his Grace's and their Lordfhips' Sentiments in this Matter, as of the laft Importance to the Welfare of the Charity Schools; and
therefore intreat all their Correfpondents to do their
utmoft to remove all Occafions of Complaint, as
they value the Profperity of thefe Schools.

The STATE of the CHARITY SCHOOLS in and about London and Westminster, according to the lateſt Accounts which have been received.

C. ſignifies Cloathed.　　　　　　*M.* Maintained.
B. Children who wear Badges on their Cloaths.　*W.* Set to work.

CHARITY SCHOOLS in the Pariſhes of	N°. of Sch.	BOYS.	GIRLS.	Boys put out ſince ſetting up of the School to — Apprenticeſhips.	Services, or taken out by Friends.	Sea.	Girls put out ſince ſetting up of the School to — Apprentices.	Service, or taken out by Friends.	No. of Children educated, cloathed, in the whole, relating to theſe two Schools in them.
Aldgate Ward With-in, formerly St. *Katharine Creed*, 1717, C. —	2	35	15	173	328	17	18	10	596
St. Alphage, London, ſet up for Boys 1751, for Girls 1753, C.B.	2	18	7						25
St. Andrew Holborn, erected 1696, C. B. —	2	80	71	912	546	86	374	884	2953
In the ſame Pariſh, 1715, for Teaching Navigation to 40 Children gratis, out of any Charity Schools within the Bills of Mortality, kept at No. 17, King's Head-c. Gough-ſq.; from whence 290 Boys have been put Apprentices to Sea, included in the Numbers put out of their reſpective Schools	—								
St Anne Alderſgate, 1709, C.B.	2	73	30	561				392	1056
Alderſgate Ward, 1702	2	30	30	571	332	10	38	412	1423
St. Anne Blackfryars, ſet up 1705, ſupported by Endowment, C.	2	51	52	409	252	26	196	359	1345
St. Anne, Soho, 1698, C.B. 10 Girls taken into the School-houſe, and wholly maintained, and when qualified put out to Service	2	80	60	439	461	26	182	513	1761
St. Anne's, Limehouſe, erected 1779 —	2	15	35	15	20	15	15	80	195
St. Anne's, Limehouſe, Poplar and Blackwall, eſtabliſhed 1711	1	50	—	638	422	62			1172
Saint Bartholomew the Great, for Boys 1717, and for Girls 1727, Pt. C.	2	36	24	197	227	23	44	254	805
Batterſea, *Surry*, founded and endowed by a Perſon of Quality for 20 Boys, taught to Read, Write, and caſt Accounts, ſeveral of whom are afterwards Apprenticed with the Intereſt of two Legacies left for that Purpoſe —	1	20	—	100	140				260
	20	488	324	4015	2728	265	867	2904	11591

CHARITY-SCHOOLS in the Parishes of	N° of Sch.	BOYS	GIRLS	Boys put out since setting up of the School to			Girls put out since setting up of the School to		No. of Children educated in the Schools, including those now in them.
				Appren-ticeships	service or taken out by Friends	Sea	Appren-tices	Services or taken out by Friends	
St. Botolph Alderfgate, 1701, C. B.	1	40	—	240	547				827
Billinfgate Ward, 1714, C.B.	1	40	—	222	630	57			949
St. Botolph Aldgate, for Boys, fet up 1688, and for Girls 1700, C. B.	2	61	40	515	257	27	21	416	1337
St. Botolph Bifhopfgate, 1702, C. B.	2	30	30						60
St. Bride's Parifh, 1711, C.	2	40	30	181	262	12	67	322	914
Bridge, Candlewick, and Dowgate Ward, for Boys 1710, Girls 1717, formerly under the Name of St. Michael Crooked-lane and St. Magnus the Martyr, C.B.	2	60	40						100
Britifh or Welch School, Gray's-inn-lane *, fet up 1718, for the Inftructing, Cloathing, and putting forth Apprentice poor Children, defcended of Welch Parents, born in or near London, that have no Parochial Settlement here	2	66	25	530	124	126	21	50	942
Broad-ftreet Ward, 1714, C. B.	2	50	30	579	984	31	9		1683
Camberwell, Surry, 1714 and 1721, C. B.	2	35	30						65
Caftlebaynard Ward, C. Boys 1710, Girls 1719	2	34	24						58
Chelfea, Middlefex, fet up 1707, endow'd with 10 l. per Ann. for ever, by the late Mr. Chamberlayne, Pt. C. and Pt. M.	2	35	20	75	12			5	147
In the fame Parifh, fet up June 1709, for Soldiers' Girls, fupported by Ladies, feven of whom are Truftees, C.	1	—	33					7	40
Chrift - Church, Spital-fields, fet up 1708, C. B.	2	50	50	211	505	22	738		1576
Chrift-Church in Surry, Boys 1711, Girls 1715, C.	2	40	40	572	436	19		634	1741
St. Clement Dane, 1702, C.	2	60	40	334	290	66	320	564	1674
	27	641	432	3459	4047	360	1176	1998	12113

* Maintained in the Houfe.

CHARITY-SCHOOLS in the Parishes of	N° of Sch.	BOYS.	GIRLS.	Apprenticeships	Boys put out since setting up of the School to — Services, or taken out by Friends	Sea.	Girls put out since setting up of the School to — Apprentices.	Services, or taken out by Friends.	No. of Children educated in the Schools, including thofe now in them.
In the fame Parifh of St. Clement Dane, an Horn-book School for Boys and Girls, 1724, Pt. C.	2	19	11						30
Coleman-ftreet Ward School, C. B.	2	40	25	230	375	27	120	103	920
Cordwainers and Bread-ftreet Ward, C. B. Boys 1701, Girls 1714	2	50	30	347	778	24	100	419	1748
Cornhill and Lime-ftreet Ward, C. B. 1710	2	45	35	306	1068	39	—	—	1493
Cripplegate Ward Without, in Redcrofs-ftreet, 1698, C.B.	2	102	100	756	1705	90	—	1365	4118
Cripplegate Ward Within, fet up 1712, in Aldermanbury	2	50	25	143	1074	4	7	377	1680
In the fame Parifh, fupported by the Legacies of Lady Elean. Holles, Ed. Buckley, John Briftow, Efqrs. & others, 1709, C.	1	—	70						70
Deptford in Kent, C.	2	50	20	8					78
St. Dunftan in the Weft, C. Boys 1708, Girls 1710	2	50	40	357	792	59	335	—	1633
St. Edmund the King. A Subfcript. and Collect. to put out Children Apprentices educated in the Charity Schools, and 240 Children have been put out, included in the Numbers put out of their refpective Schools	—	—	240						240
St. Ethelburga, C.B. fet up B. 1719, G. 1774, firft in the Parifh of St. Mary Abchurch, fupported by the Subfcriptions of a Society, and other Collections	2	36	20	246	418	14	—	66	800
Farringdon Ward Within, fet up 1705, C. B.	2	60	40	233	127	51	187	101	799
French Charity - School, Spitalfields	2	14	17						31
Finfbury Charity-School, fet up 1792	2	30	15	20	4	—	4	—	73
	25	546	448	2886	6341	308	753	2131	13413

CHARITY-SCHOOLS in the Parishes of	Nº of Sch.	BOYS.	GIRLS.	Boys put out since setting up of the School to			Girls put out since setting up of the School to		No. of Children educated in the Schools, including those now in them.
				Apprenticeships.	Services, or taken out by Friends.	S.a.	Apprentices.	Services, or taken out by Friend.	
St. George, *Middlesex*, or Rayne's Hospital, C. Boys 1716, Girls 1719. ☞ *See below.*	2	50	90	279				452	871
St. George the Martyr, 1708, C. B.	2	40	30	447			200		717
St. George Southwark, B. 1715, C. Girls 1747	2	40	25						65
Sir *George Wheeler's* Chapel in *Spital-Fields*, 1703, C. W.	1	36							36
St.Giles in the Fields, and St. George Bloomsbury, set up 1705, C. The Trustees of these Schools, in 1728, finding themselves burdened with binding out Girls to Trades, agreed that for the future 16 of the eldest Girls should be wholly maintained in the Schools, with a Person appointed to teach them what is necessary to qualify them for Services	2	101	70	805	627	20	398	267	2288
Greenwich, *Kent*, 1700, C.W. the Children here spin, and make their own Cloaths, both Linen and Woollen	1	40		4	200				244
In the same Parish, cloathed in Green	1	20							20
In the same Parish, cloathed in Grey	1	50							50
Hammersmith, *Middlesex*	2	20	20						40
Highgate, *Middlesex*, C. set up for Girls 1722. The Schoolhouse was built by Edward Pauncefoot, Esq; who endowed it with 5 l. per ann. for ever	1		20						20
St. James, Clerkenwell, C. B. 1700	2	60	40						100
In the same Parish, 1730, for Children 5 years old, to qualify them for the other Schools	2	20	10						30
Peter Joys, Esq; set up June 29, 1705, by Peter Joys, Esq;	2	37	24						61
St. James Westminster, C. supported by the Offertory, 1697	2	80	50	261				524	915
	23	594	379	1796	827	20	1122	719	5457

☞ RAYNE's Hospital, set up in the same Parish of St. George in the East, 1736, for 40 GIRLS. These Girls, being transplanted from the Parish School into the said Hospital, are entirely maintained and trained up for Services.—After the Age of 22, Six of them, producing Certificates of their good Behaviour during their Servitude, draw Lots, twice in the Year, for a Marriage-Portion of 100 l. to settle them in the World with an honest industrious Mechanic.—58 have received it, and 379 have been educated since its Institution.

CHARITY-SCHOOLS in the Parishes of	No. of Sch.	BOYS.	GIRLS.	Boys put out since fitting up of the School to			Girls put out since letting up of the School to		No. of Children in the Schools, including thof. now in them.
				Apprenticeships	Services, or taken out by Friends	Sea.	Apprentices	Services, including or taken out by Friends	
In the fame Parish, in King-*street*, fet up in 1712, by the late Archbishop *Tenison*, supported out of the Revenue of the Chapel, *C.*	2	36	120						156
In the fame Parish of St. *James Westminster*, fet up 1725, *C. M. W.* to prepare them for Service, supported by Collections at Sermons, and cafual Benefactions	1	70		626					696
St. John at *Hackney*, *C.* fet up 1714, laid down *Lady-day* 1735, revived *Midsummer* following	2	30	30						60
St. John *Wapping*, fet up for Boys 1704, Girls 1708, *C.*	2	50	40	482		205	2	484	1263
St. John *South.* 1735, *C.* * separated from St. Olave South.	1		36					404	440
St. James *Clerkenwell,C.* 1767	2	60	40	270				404	774
Isleworth, *Middlesex*, 1715 *C. W.*	2	40	20						60
St. Katherine *near the* Tower, 1707, *C.*	2	35	15	28	290	158		207	733
Kenfington, *Mid.* 1707. To which HIS MAJESTY is gracioufly pleafed to allow 80 *l. per Ann.* and the Children have a Dinner every Sunday from *Michaelmas* to *Lady-day*	2	30	20	82	15		35	53	235
Lambeth in *Surry*, Boys 1708, Girls 1706, *C. W.* the Girls are employed in Knitting and Sewing	1	50							50
Langbourn Ward, fet up in the Name of *Alhallows Lombard-street*, 1702, and made the Ward School 1735, *C. B.*	1	60		379	717	16			1172
St. Leonard *Shoreditch*, Boys erected 1705, Girls, 1709, *C. B.*	2	60	50	435	499	12	97	640	1795
St. Luke *Middlesex*, from the Parish of St. *Giles Cripplegate*, fet up 1710, Girls 1761, *C. B.*	2	100	50	647					797
	22	621	421	2949	1521	391	134	2192	8229

* The Truftees have taken 14 into the Houfe, wholly to be maintained.

O

CHARITY-SCHOOLS in the Parishes of	N° of Sch.	BOYS.	GIRLS.	Boys put out since setting up of the School to			Girls put out since setting up of the School to		No. of Children educated in the Schools, including those now in them.
				Apprenticeships	Services, or taken out by Friends	Sea.	Apprentices	Services, or taken out by Friends	
In the same Parish, C. set up 1727, supported by a Legacy of Mr. *John Fuller*, deceased; and Five Pounds allowed to put out each Boy Apprentice	1	20	—	46	39				105
St. Margaret Westminster, cloathed in Blue, the Boys set up 1683, the Girls 1714, *W.* Being the first Institution of this Kind against Popery	2	52	34	528	190	50	84	239	1177
In the same Parish, cloathed in Grey, *W.* and *M.* the Boys set up 1698	2	50	36	381				218	685
St. Martin in the Fields 1699, C. In these Schools 35 Girls are *M.* and one third Part of the Boys are daily employed in useful Labour, so that the whole School works 2 Days in a Week, by Rotation	2	80	40						120
St. Mary Islington, 1710. *C.B.*	2	36	24	329	84	4	16	133	626
St. Mary Magdalene Bermondsey, Boys 1711, Girls 1722, *C.*	2	50	30						80
St. Mary Overee, *alias* St. Saviour Southwark, *C.*	2	60	50					206	316
St. Mary Rotherhith, 1739	2	25	20	175	104			100	424
In the same Parish, *C.* Boys set up 1741, Girls 1746	2	16	20						36
In the same Parish, not Cloathed, 1755	2	25	15	160	41			75	316
St. Mary-le-bone, cloathed, set up 1750 *	2	50	44	425	100		192	93	904
Do. Sch. of Industry, 1791	2	40	16		164			72	292
St. Mary le Strand, 1708, *C.*	1	20	—	176	250	6			452
St. Mary Whitechapel, 1705, *C.*	2	60	40	4				2	106
St Matthew, Bethn. Green Girls set up 1762, Boys 1765, *C.*	2	30	30		259			306	625
Mile End, Old Town, set up 1723, *C.*	2	30	20	105			1		156
In the same Parish, cloathed in Blue, and endowed	1	—	100						100
Mortlake in *Surry*, set up 1721, *C.*	2	9	9						18
Newington Butts, *Surry*, 1710, *C.*	2	30	20	74	406			80	610
Norton Falgate, School for Boys 1691, Girls 1703, and has been very useful as a Nursery to the neighbouring Charity Schools	1	36							36
	36	719	548	2403	1637	61	294	1522	7184

* They are boarded, lodged in the House, and every Necessary found.
† Fifty are cloathed from their own Industry.

CHARITY-SCHOOLS in the Parishes of	N° of Sch.	BOYS.	GIRLS.	Apprenticeships	Services or taken out by Friends.	Sea.	Apprentices.	Services, or taken out by Friends	No. of Children educated in the Schools, including those now in them.
St. Olave, South. 1735, C.	1	40	—	7	28				75
St. Paul Covent-garden, Boys or Girls 1713, C.	2	*20	20	225	291	10	115	198	879
St. Paul Shadwell, Boys 1699, Girls 1712, C.	2	45	35	346	758	67	38	526	1815
St. Pancras, set up 1786	1	—	40					97	137
Pentonville, 1788, C.	2	12	12	25	6			21	76
Queen-Hithe Ward, set up in 1717, Cl. B.	2	24	24	359				296	703
Radcliff Hamlet, Stepney, Boys 1710, Girls 1723	2	35	15	100			262		412
Richmond in Surry, set up 1713, C.	1	80	50	262	12	8	200	38	650
St Sepulchre London, set up 1700, C.	1	51	—	1058	56	17			1182
In the same Parish the Ladies' School, 40 boarded in the House, set up 1702, C.	1	—	51					1001	1052
In the same Parish Middle. Girls, 4 boarded in the House, set up 1711, C.	1		21						21
In the same Parish Middle. set up 1706, C.	1	30							30
Saint Stephen Walbrook, 1698 and 1778, Cl.	2	50	30	284		7		59	430
Saint Thomas Southwark, 1704, Cl.	1	30							30
Tower Ward, Girls 1707, Boys 1709, C.	2	60	60	78	1011	130	186	1148	2673
Vintry Ward, 1710, C. B.	1	50		228	789	16			1083
Wandsworth, Surry	1	25							25
Westminster French Charity-school, set up 1747	2	19	18	92	45	1	98	304	577
	26	571	376	3064	2996	256	899	3688	11850
Brought from Page 96	20	488	324	4015	2728	265	867	2904	11591
—— from Page 9-	27	641	432	3459	4047	360	1176	1998	12113
—— from Page 98	25	546	446	2386	6341	308	753	2131	13413
—— from Page 99	23	594	3-9	1796	827	20	1122	719	5457
—— from Page 100	22	621	421	2949	1521	391	134	2192	8229
—— from Page 101	36	719	546	2403	1637	61	294	1522	7184
TOTAL	179	4180	2928	20572	20097	1661	5245	15154	69837

* 14 Boys and 14 Girls are maintained in the House.
† The Boys are employed in braiding Nets for the Free British Fishery.
‡ For the Instructing, Cloathing, Maintaining, and putting forth Apprentice poor Children descended of French Protestant Refugees, born in or near London, that have no Parochial Settlement here. This School is appointed by Act of Parliament ... scriptions and Voluntary Contributions; and the Children being all taught to read and write English equally as well as French, are hereby recommended to those Masters and Mistresses, that have need of servants capable of speaking both tongues fluently. The school is kept in Windmill-street, near Tottenham-court-road.

Boys at School   —   4180 }
Girls   —   —   2928 } 7108 Total of Children at School.

Boys put out to Appren. 20572 ⎤
———— to Services, &c. 20097 ⎬ 42330 ⎫
———— Sea   -   1661 ⎭   ⎬ 69837
Girls put out to Appren. 5245 ⎤ 20399 ⎭
———— to Services, &c. 15154 ⎦

{ Total of Children put to Apprenticeships and Services, or taken out by Friends; of which 1370 are gone to Sea, out of 45 Schools. }

Note, *The* TRUSTEES *of fome Schools have thought fit to leffen the Number of Children taught in them, that the reft might be entirely fupported; which is the Reafon the Number now taught, is fhort of what it was formerly.*

The Number of CHARITY-SCHOOLS *in each County of* England *and* Wales, *with the Number of Children taught in them, according to the beft Information that has been given to the Publifher hereof, is as follows:*

	Sch.	Boys.	Girls.		Sch.	Boys.	Girls.
Anglefea	3	40		Lincolnfhire	91	1164	95
Bedfordfhire	34	345	57	Merionethfhire	2	40	22
Berkfhire	59	807	140	Middlefex	29	410	220
Brecknockfhire	5	251	47	Monmouthfhire	7	104	13
Buckinghamfhire	57	689	46	Montgomeryfhire	6	76	16
Cambridgefhire	36	673	124	Norfolk	34	570	220
Cardiganfhire	1	10		Northamptonfhire	47	508	143
Carmarthenfhire	11	121	4	Northumberland	10	430	40
Carnarvonfhire	3	35		Nottinghamfhire	30	252	28
Chefhire	17	124	66	Oxfordfhire	23	366	106
Cornwall	13	72	34	Pembrokefhire			
Cumberland	6	160	30	Radnorfhire	3	60	
Denbighhire	5	100	3	Rutlandfhire	6	32	12
Derbyfhire	18	274	51	Shropfhire	22	373	37
Devonfhire	41	679	235	Somerfetfhire	33	582	90
Dorfetfhire	13	117	29	Staffordfhire	14	230	88
Durham	12	276	20	Suffolk	40	600	140
Effex	37	498	178	Surry	29	546	144
Flintfhire	1	60		Suffex	23	512	60
Glamorganfhire	6	50		Warwickfhire	36	385	165
Gloucefterfhire	62	940	100	Weftmorland	1	16	10
Hampfhire	39	541	112	Wiltfhire	37	736	57
Herefordfhire	29	468	79	Worcefterfhire	38	612	100
Hertfordfhire	38	652	126	Yorkfhire	54	893	191
Huntingdonfhire	25	282	20				
Kent	62	963	315		615	9497	3997
Lancafhire	21	311	231	Brought forward	689	9825	3877
Leicefterfhire	30	451	30				
Carried forward	689	9825	3877		1304	19322	3874

N. B. The Society will be much obliged to fuch of their Members, as are concerned in the Support or Management of any of thefe Country Charity-Schools, to inform them of any Errors they may difcover in the above Lift; as there is Reafon to believe it is not now a correct one.

[109]

A Summary View of the CHARITY-SCHOOLS *in* Great-Britain *and* Ireland.

	Sch.	Boys.	Girls.
AT *LONDON*	179	4180	2928
In other Parts of *South-Britain*	1329	19506	3915
In *North-Britain*, by the Account publifhed in 1786	135	5187	2618
In *IREL IND*, for teaching to Read and Write only	168	2406	600
In ditto, erected purfuant to his Majefty's *Charter*, and encouraged by his Royal Bounty of 1000 *l.* per *Annum*, for inftructing, employing, and wholly maintaining the Children, exclufive of the *Dublin* Work-houfe School	42	1935	—
Total of *Schools*	1851	33214	10061
		10061	
Boys and *Girls* now taught in thofe *Schools*		43275	

Note, Where the Number of Scholars has been fignified to the Publifher of this Account, without diftinguifhing the *Sexes*, they are put in the *Column* of *Boys*.

___

A PROPOSAL *made by the* SOCIETY *to the* Truftees *of the* CHARITY-SCHOOLS, *for adding* Work *to the* Learning *ufually given to the* Children.

THE Inftructing of Youth, and Providing for the Poor and Impotent, are fuch obvious Duties, that they meet with univerfal Approbation; but the moft proper Means to attain that good End are often difputed.

THE Erecting of Charity-Schools has moft certainly laid a good Foundation for the firft; and the late excellent Law relating to *Work-Houfes*, has put it in the Power of every Parifh in a much better Manner to provide for the latter.

As to the Charity-Schools, it muft needs be acknowledged, that thofe excellent Perfons who firft

3   formed,

formed, and they who have fince conducted that good Work, ought ever to be mentioned with Honour: And now, that fuch Schools are eftablilhed in moft Parts of the Kingdom, it is much to be wifhed that fome Means could be contrived to render them ftill more ufeful, and effectually to anfwer the good Pur-pofes of their Inftitution.

IT is conceived, that if the Children educated in Charity-Schools were employed in fome fuch Bufi-nefs as they are capable of, it would be no Hindrance to their Learning, and might have a very good Effect, by inuring them early to Induftry; but what that Employment fhould be, and the Manner of conduct-ing it, muft be left to the Managers of the feveral Schools, who are the beft Judges of what is moft proper and convenient to be done.

SUPPOSE *England* and *Wales* to contain *Ten Thou-fand* Parifhes, and that but *Ten* Perfons in every Parifh, one with another, were by fome Method employed, who were perfectly idle before, then the whole Number of Perfons fo fet to work would be *One Hundred Thoufand*, and, if they work but 300 Days in a Year, and one with another earned but a *Half-Penny* a Day, the Produce of their Labour at the Year's End would amount to 62,500 Pounds.

Coarfe Wool, Flax, or Hemp to be fpun in the Charity-Schools.

THE Spinning of coarfe Wool, Flax or Hemp, is a Thing eafily learnt, and the Wafte which will be always made by Beginners will not amount to much. And if it were poflible fo to contrive it, that the Pa-rents of the Children might reap fome Advantage from what is fo earned, it would be a great Induce-ment for them to keep the Children to their Bufinefs; and if the Undertaking fucceeded, it is to be hoped, that many good People would fend in coarfe Meterials to be worked up for the Benefit of the School.

9   IT

I T is impoffible to give minute and particular
Directions for conducting this Undertaking, and
therefore that muft be left to the Managers, who
will beft judge what is neceffary to be done; but
till the School is very well got into fome Method,
the beft Way will moft certainly be to keep the Bufinefs in a fmall Compafs.

THo' the Spinning of Wool, and Flax, or Hemp,
is propofed, as moft advantageous, yet where this
is found impracticable, the Children fhould be employed in fome other Way, and always have what
they earn for their Encouragement: That would
make them diligent, and induce all good Chriftians
to affift in an Undertaking, which fo much con-
duces to the Glory of GoD, and the Good of Mankind.

There having fometimes happened much Difficulty in obtaining a Legacy given to the Charity-Schools, by reafon of fome Defect in ex-
preffing fuch Bequeft; it feems convenient to fet down how fuch Legacy may be fo expreffed, as to prevent any Scruple about paying
it; which may be done in this Manner, *viz.*

I T E M, *I* A. B. *do give and bequeath unto*
G. H. *of* the
Sum *of* Pounds,
*to the Intent, and on Truft, that he do pay the fame
to the Treafurers for the Time being of the* Charity-
School, *for Teaching* [poor Children, *or* poor Boys,
or poor Girls,] *to Read,* &c. *in the Parifh of*
in the City
of or in the
County *of* for the
Ufe of the faid School.

Λ L E T-

A

L E T T E R
O F

DR. E D M U N D G I B S O N,
Late Lord Bifhop of *L O N D O N,*

TO THE

C L E R G Y OF HIS D I O C E S E,

Dated *Whitehall, April* 3, 1740.

·GOOD BROTHER,

THE Decay of Piety and Religion, and the Increafe of Sin and Vice, are fo vifible in our Days, notwithftanding the Endeavours of the Parochial Clergy to prevent them ; that no additional·Expedients ought to be omitted, which may help, in any Meafure, to preferve among our People. a Senfe of Duty, and a Spirit of Devotion.

ONE of thefe Expedients is, the putting into their Hands, 'as Occafion fhall be found, fome fhort and plain Tracts upon Religious Subjects ; fuch as being fhort, they are like to read, or may eafily procure to be read to them ; and being alfo plain, they cannot fail of underftanding ; and moreover, being always at Hand, and read over often, they will naturally make a *deeper Impreffion* upon their Minds, than Inftructions and Admonitions, either from the Pulpit, or by Word of Mouth.

IT was with this View, that feveral Bifhops, Clergymen, and other ferious Perfons among the Laity, did long fince form themfelves into a Society, for printing and difperfing fuch practical Tracts in great Numbers. And for the difperfing them more effectually, they have from Time to Time admitted, and continue to admit, feveral Perfons in all Parts of the Kingdom, whom they call CORRESPONDING MEMBERS ; and who are intitled to have a Supply of them, to be difpofed of among fuch of the neighbouring Clergy or Laity as defire them ; the Bound Books, mentioned in their Catalogue, at the prime Coft in *Quires,* the Society

ciety being at the Charge of Binding; and the Stitch'd Books,
at one *half* of what is set down as the prime Cost of each; the
other half of the Charge being borne by the standing Subscriptions
of the Members of the Society, and by other occasional Benefactions. And the Privilege of sending for, and receiving those
Books and small Tracts, on the Terms before-mentioned, is common to all the CORRESPONDING MEMBERS, as such, whether
they be SUBSCRIBERS or not; on Account of the Trouble they
are content to take in answering the great Ends of the Society, by
conveying their Tracts into many Hands, and on the same easy
Terms; without any Advantage to themselves, besides the Pleasure
of doing good.

THIS Society has subsisted many Years, under the Name of
The Society for Promoting Christian Knowledge. And as, by their
Endeavours in that Way, great Good has been already done to
Religion, so much more would probably be done, if the Design,
and their Methods of carrying it on, were more generally under-
stood and attended to. And because some of the Clergy may not
know that there is such a Society, and many others may be unac-
quainted with the true End and Manner of it; I desire that those
in your Neighbourhood may have this Account of it communicated
to them, as you have Opportunity. At the same Time it is left
to every one's Judgment, how far he has *Occasion*, within his own
Cure, for such Assistances as these, to co-operate with his own
Pastoral Labours.

I AM not without Hope, that when this Method of doing Service
to Religion is known and considered, Persons who are of Ability,
both among the Clergy and Laity, will be disposed to become
subscribing Members, or occasional Contributors; for the better
Support of the Society in carrying on the Work, and to make
the good Effects of it more and more extensive. And so, com-
mending you and your Labours to the Blessing of God,

I remain, Sir,

Your faithful Friend and Brother,

E D M. L O N D O N.

P   Nº III.

Nº III.

A
CATALOGUE OF THE BOOKS
DISPERSED BY THE
SOCIETY,

Which may be had by their M E M B E R S on the Terms
herein set forth.

The Articles † have been admitted into the Catalogue within the laſt Year.

I. *The Books here underwritten are all bound at the Expence of the
Society, and the Members are only charged with the Payment of ſuch Sums as are placed oppoſite to each Book* *.

1. Bibles *at the following Prices, viz.*

		s.	d.
T HE *Oxford* Bible, Pica Character, with Marginal Re-ferences, in Medium 4to. - - - }		15	6
The ſame, on fine Royal Paper - - -		1·11	0
The *Oxford* Bible, Brevier Character, with Marginal Re-ferences, ſingle, in 8vo. - - }		6	0
The ſame, ————— with the Apocrypha -		7	0
The ſame, on a Crown Paper, without Marginal References, in 8vo.		4	0
The ſame, ————— with the Apocrypha		4	10
The ſame, ————— with Service, Pſalms, and Apocrypha		6	0
The ſame, ————— Service and Pſalms, no Apocrypha		5	2
The ſame, — Minion Character, ſingle, in 12mo. - - -		3	0
The ſame, ———— with the Apocrypha - - - -		3	9
The ſame, ———— with the Service, Pſalms, and the Apocrypha		4	6
The ſame, ———— with Service and Pſalms, no Apocrypha -		3	9
The ſame, Nonpareil, ſingle, in 12mo. - - - -		2	0
The ſame, ————— with Service and Pſalms - - -		2	8
The ſame, ————— ſingle 24to. - - - - -		2	0

The

	l.	s.	d.
The *Cambridge* Bible, Pica Character, with Marginal References, in Medium 4*to.*		15	6
The fame, on fine Royal Paper		1	11	0
The *Cambridge* Bible, Brevier, with Marginal References, fingle, in 8*vo.*		6	0
The fame, ————————— with the Apocrypha		7	0
The fame, on a Crown Paper, without Marginal References, in 8*vo.*		4	0
The fame, ———————— with the Apocrypha		4	10
The fame, ————————— with Service, Pfalms, and Apocrypha		6	0
The fame, ———————— Service, Pfalms, and no Apocrypha		5	2
The fame, Minion, fingle, in 12*mo.*		3	0
The fame, ——————— with the Apocrypha		3	9
The fame, ——————— with the Service, Pfalms, and Apocrypha		4	6
The fame, ——————— with Service and Pfalms, and no Apocrypha		3	9
The fame, Nonpareil, fingle, in 12*mo.*		2	0
The fame, ——————— with Service and Pfalms		2	8
The fame, ——— fingle, 24*to.*		2	0

2. Teftaments *and* Pfalter, *at the following Prices,* viz.

	s.	d.
Teftament, Pica Character, 8*vo.*	1	7
——————— Long Primer, 8*vo.*	0	11
——————— Brevier, 12*mo.*	0	7½
——————— Nonpareil, 24*to.*	0	7½
The New Teftament in *French,* 12*mo.*	1	6
Pfalter, with the Collects, and Communion Service, 12*mo.*	0	5

3. Common Prayers, *with* Pfalms.

	s.	d.
The *Oxford* Common Prayer, Pica 8*vo.* with the *Old* Verfion of Pfalms	2	4
The fame, with Companion to the Altar	2	7
The fame, with the *New* Verfion of Pfalms and Hymns	2	8
The fame, with Companion to the Altar	2	11
The fame, Brevier 12*mo.* with the *Old* Verfion of Pfalms	1	3
The fame, with Companion to the Altar	1	4½
The fame, with the *New* Verfion of Pfalms	1	5½
The fame, with Companion to the Altar	1	6½
The fame, with the Extracts from the *New* Verfion of Pfalms	1	3½
The fame, with Companion to the Altar	1	4½

P 2

The

		s.	d.
The fame,	Minion 12mo. with the *Old* Version of Psalms	1	0½
The fame,	with Companion to the Altar	1	2
The fame,	with the *New* Version of Psalms	1	2
The fame,	with Companion to the Altar	1	3
The fame,	with the Extracts from the *New* Version of Psalms	1	0½
The fame,	with the Companion to the Altar	1	1½
The fame,	Long Lines, 12mo. on a fine Paper, with the *Old* Version of Psalms	2	2
The fame,	without Psalms	1	10
The fame,	Nonpareil 24to. with the *Old* Version of Psalms	0	9½
The fame,	with the Extracts from the *New* Version of Psalms	0	9
The fame,	with the *New* Version of Psalms	0	11
The *Cambridge* Common Prayer, Pica 8vo. with the *Old* Version of Psalms		2	4
The fame,	with Companion to the Altar	2	7
The fame,	with the *New* Version of Psalms	2	8
The fame,	with the New Version, and Companion to the Altar	2	11
The fame,	Long Primer 12mo. with the *Old* Version of Psalms	1	8
The fame,	with Companion to the Altar	1	9½
The fame,	with the *New* Version of Psalms	1	9½
The fame,	with the New Version, and Companion to the Altar	1	10½
The fame,	Brevier 12mo. with the *Old* Version of Psalms	1	3
The fame,	with Companion to the Altar	1	4½
The fame,	with the *New* Version of Psalms	1	5½
The fame,	with Companion to the Altar	1	6½
The fame,	with the Extracts from the *New* Version of Psalms	1	8½
The fame,	with the Companion to the Altar	1	4½
The fame,	Minion 12mo. with the *Old* Version of Psalms	1	0½
The fame,	with Companion to the Altar	1	2
The fame,	with the *New* Version of Psalms	1	2
The fame,	with Companion to the Altar	1	3
The fame,	with the Extracts from the *New* Version of Psalms	1	0½
The fame,	with the Companion to the Altar	1	1½
The fame,	Long Lines, 12mo. on a fine Paper, with the *Old* Version of Psalms	2	2
The fame,	without Psalms	1	10
The fame,	Nonpareil 24to. with the *Old* Version of Psalms	0	9½
The fame,	with the *New* Version of Psalms	0	11
The fame,	with the Extracts from the New Version of Psalms	0	9

The

	s.	*d.*
The Common Prayer in *Welch*, Long Primer 12*mo.* with the *Old* Verfion of Pfalms - - - - - -	1	10
The *New* Verfion of Pfalms, by *Tate* and *Brady*, with the Hymns, in 8*vo.* - - - - - - -	1	6
The fame, Brevier 12*mo.* - - - - -	0	8½
The fame, Minion 12*mo.* - - - - -	0	7½
The fame, Nonpareil 24*to.* - - - - -	0	7½
Extracts from the *New* Verfion of the Pfalms for the Ufe of Parifh Churches, Brevier 12*mo.* - - - -	0	5
The fame, Minion 12*mo.* - - - -	0	5
The fame, Nonpareil, 24*to.* - - - - -	0	4

N. B. The *New Verfion of the Pfalms* by *Tate* and *Brady*, and the Extracts from the *New Verfion*, will be allowed to Members at Half Price, when bound up with the *Common Prayer Books.*

Other RELIGIOUS BOOKS *bound at the Expence of the* Society, *which are charged to the Members only at the Price fet againft each Book.*

4. On *the* Holy Scriptures.

	s.	*d.*
Gaftrel's (Bifhop) Chriftian Inftitutes, 12*mo.* - -	1	6
Greenwood's (Dr.) Harmony of the Four Gofpels, 12*mo.*	1	6
The Four Gofpels and the Acts of the Apoftles; with Notes explanatory and practical, for the Ufe of Families and Schools; by *Ifaac Mann*, D. D. late Lord Bifhop of *Cork* and *Rofs*	2	6
Oftervald's Arguments on the Books and Chapters of the Old and New Teftament: With Practical Obfervations, and a Preliminary Difcourfe. In Two large Vols. 8*vo.* a new Edition	11	0
Sellon's Abridgment of the Holy Scriptures, 12*mo.* - -	0	10
The fame, tranflated into *French* - - - - -	1	0
Trimmer's (Mrs.) Abridgment of Scripture Hiftory; confifting of Leffons felected from the Old Teftament, for the Ufe of Charity Schools, Kitchens, and Cottages - - -	1	3
————Abridgment of the New Teftament on the fame Plan -	0	11
———— Scripture Catechifm, Part I. containing a familiar Explanation of the Leffons felected from the Old Teftament. For the Ufe of Schools and Families - - - -	2	0
———— Scripture Catechifm, Part II. containing a familiar Explanation of the Leffons felected from the Writings of the Four Evangelifts. For the Ufe of Schools and Families	2	0

5. On *the* Church Catechifm.

	s.	*d.*
Duke's Lectures on the Chriftian Covenant, on the Articles of the Chriftian Faith, and on the two Sacraments, 12*mo.* -	1	0

Kenn's

6. On the Chriftian Religion, Doctrine and Practice.

• Either of thefe three Tracts may be had feparate, as fee Page 125.

* *This Article is alfo in the Lift of Tracts, fee Page 120.*

6   10. MIS-

10. MISCELLANIES.

	s.	*d.*
Worthington (Dr.) on Self-Refignation, 12*mo.* - -	1	0
Peers's Companion for the Aged, 12*mo.* - -	0	3

II. *All the Stitched Books in the remaining Part of this Catalogue are allowed to the* Members *at half of the Price fet down againft the Title of each Book, the* Society *defraying the other half of the Charge.* —*And fuch as are of a larger Size, the* SOCIETY *is alfo at the Expence of Half-binding, and they are marked with an* *.

1. On the Holy Scriptures.

	Single.	Hunt.
	d.	*s. d.*
* PLAIN Directions for Reading the Holy Scriptures -	1½	10 0
Several Methods of Reading the Holy Scriptures in private	1¼	7 0
Oftervald's Neceffity and Ufefulnefs of Reading the Holy Scriptures - - - - - - -	2	14 0
——— Abridgment of the Hiftory of the Bible -	1	5 6

2. Publick and Private DEVOTION.

	d.	*s. d.*
* *Beft's* (Dr.) Effay on the Daily Service of the Church of England, recommending an Attendance upon it -	6	48 0
Beveridge's (Bifhop) Sermon on the Common Prayer -	2¼	19 0
* *Brockwell's* Practical Expofition of the Lord's Prayer; confidered as defigned for Inftruction as well as Ufe ; as a Rule of Duty, as well as a Form of Prayer - - -	6	42 0
The Chriftian's Daily Devotion, with Directions how to walk with God all the Day long - -	1	6 0
The Collects taken from the Book of Common Prayer, 1 *s.* 3*d.* per Dozen, or - - - - - - -	1¼	9 0

Directions

Q   The

	Single.	Hund.
	d.	s. d.

3. CATECHISM.

The Church Catechism on a Pasteboard - -	1	6 0
Church Catechism broke into short Questions - -	1¼	8 0
The same with the Answers at length instead of References by Figures - - - - -	2	12 0
* Mann's (Bishop) Exposition of the Church Catechism -	3	20 0
* The Catechism briefly explained by short Notes, grounded upon Holy Scripture, *commonly called the* Oxford *Catechism*	4½	36 0

4. CONFIRMATION.

The Order of Confirmation, with Instructions for them that come to be confirmed, and Prayers to be used before and after Confirmation - -	1½	10 0
Nelson's Instructions for them that come to be Confirmed	1½	10 0
Pastoral Advice before Confirmation - - -	1½	10 0
Pastoral Advice after Confirmation - - -	1	5 0
Adams's(Dr.)Pastoral Advice to Young Persons before Confirmation	2	12 0
The same in *French* - - - - - -	2	12 0
The same in *Welch* - - - - -	2	10 0
Nowell's Earnest Exhortation to Young Persons lately confirmed - - - - - -	2	12 0
Secker's (Archbishop) Sermon on Confirmation -	2	12 0

5. BAPTISM.

Serious Address to Godfathers and Godmothers - -	1¼	8 0
Bradford (Bishop) on Baptismal and Spiritual Regeneration	1¼	10 0

6. *The* HOLY COMMUNION.

An Admonition on the Holy Sacrament, on a Sheet -	gratis	
The same, in *Welch* - - - - -	ditto	
Barrow's (Dr. *Isaac*) Doctrine of the Sacraments -	3	20 0
* A Friendly Call to the Holy Communion, wherein is shewn to the meanest Capacity, the Nature and End of the Lord's Supper, with a particular Address to Servants. To which are added Prayers, Meditations, &c. - - -	5	40 0
* A Companion to the Altar - - - -	2½	20 0

* *Fleetwood's*

Q 2

8. Concerning Particular Duties.

The

9. COMMON VICES.

	Single.	Hund.
	d.	s. d.

An Earneſt and Affectionate Addreſs to the common People, concerning their uſual Recreations on *Shrove* Tueſday — 0½ | 4 0
Elleſby's Caution againſt Ill Company - - - 1¼ | 10 0
An Exerciſe againſt Lying -- - - 1 | 4 0
Finch's (Dr.) Conſiderations on the Uſe and Abuſe of Oaths judicially taken - - - - 2 | 14 0
Fleetwood (Biſhop) againſt Swearing - - 1 | 8 0
Gibſon's (Bp.) Admonition againſt Profane and Common Swearing 1 | 7 0
——— Earneſt Diſſuaſive from Intemperance in Meats and Drinks: To which is added, An Appendix, with a View more particularly to Spirituous Liquors - - - 2 | 13 0
——— Evil and Danger of Lukewarmneſs in Religion - 1 | 7 6
Pearce's (Biſhop) Sermon againſt Self-Murder - - 2 | 12 0
Stonhouſe's (Sir *James*) Admonitions againſt Drunkenneſs, Swearing, and Sabbath-Breaking - - 1 | 6 0
The ſame on a broad Sheet - - - *gratis*
The ſame, in Welch - - - - ditto
Woodward's (Dr.) Kind Caution to Profane Swearers - 0¼ | 3 0
——— Baſeneſs of Slandering and Backbiting - 1 | 6 0
——— Diſſuaſive from Gaming - - - 1 | 5 0
——— Diſſuaſive from Drunkenneſs - - - 0¼ | 4 6
——— Grievous Scandal of Profane Language - - 0¼ | 4 6
White's Diſſuaſive from Stealing - - - - 1¼ | 10 0

10. Education *and* Inſtruction *of* Children *and* Families.

An Account of the Chief Truths of the Chriſtian Religion - 1 | 5 0
An Addreſs to the Parents of Children attending Sunday Schools, on a Sheet. *Gratis.*
* *Brooke's* (*William*, Eſq;) Short Addreſſes to the Children of Sunday Schools, on particular Texts of Scripture - 6 | 48 0
* *Waldo's* (*Pete*, Eſq;) Admonitions for Children in Sunday Schools 6 | 48 0
Child's Firſt Book, 1s. 3d. per Dozen, or - - - 1½ | 9 0
The Child's Firſt Book, Part the Second - - - 1 | 8 0
* *Fox's* Leſſons for Children - - - - - 3 | 24 0
* *Kennet's* (Biſhop) Chriſtian Scholar, or Directions for Youth 2¼ | 18 0
Regular Method of Governing a Family - - - 1 | 8 0
Orders to be read and given to the Parents, on the Admittance of their Children into the Charity-Schools, on a Sheet ½ | 4 0

	Single.	Hund.
	d.	*s. d.*

Stonhoufe's (Sir *James*) Religious Inftruction of Children recommended - - - - - - - - - } 3 | 20 0

Trimmer's (Mrs.) Charity School Spelling Book, Part I. containing the Alphabet, Spelling Leffons, and Short Stories of Good and Bad Boys, in Words of one Syllable only } 2 | 14 0

The fame, with Stories of Good and Bad Girls - - 2 | 14 0

*——— Charity School Spelling Book, Part II. containing Words divided into Syllables, Leffons with Scripture Names, &c. - - - - - - - } 6 | 42 0

Wilfon's (Bifhop) True Chriftian Method of educating Children - - - - - - - - - } 1½ | 9 0

11. AGAINST POPERY.

Gibfon's (Bifhop) Danger and Mifchiefs of Popery - - 1 | 6 6

* A brief Confutation of the Errors of the Church of *Rome*, extracted from Archbifhop *Secker*'s five Sermons againft Popery, and publifhed by the Right Rev. Bifhop *Porteus*, for the Ufe of the Diocefe of *Chefter* - } 6 | 42 0

Porteus's (Bifhop) Letter to the Clergy of the Diocefe of *Chefter*, containing Precautions refpecting the *Roman* Catholics - - - - - - - } 2 | 12 0

A Proteftant Catechifm, fhewing the principal Errors of the Church of *Rome* - - - - } 1½ | 10 0

Queftions and Anfwers concerning the refpective Tenets of the Church of *England*, and that of *Rome* - - } 1 | 7 0

* *Synge*'s (Archbifhop) St. *Paul*'s Defcription of his own Religion 3 | 22 0

* ——————— Charitable Addrefs to all that are of the Communion of the Church of *Rome* - - - } 5 | 40 0

——————— Sincere Chriftian and Convert from the Church of *Rome*, exemplified in the Life of *Daniel Herley*, a poor *Irifh* Peafant - - - - - } 2½ | 19 0

Tillotfon's (Archbifhop) Diffuafive from Popery, in a Letter to the Right Honourable *Charles* then Earl and afterwards Duke of *Shrewfbury* - - - - - } 3 | 20 0

* ——————— Difcourfe againft Tranfubftantiation 1½ | 14 0

A View of the Articles of the *Proteftant* and *Popifh* Faith - 0½ | 6 0

12. ENTHU-

12. ENTHUSIASM.

An Earneſt and Affectionate Addreſs to *Methodiſts*   1 10 0
Gibſon's (Biſhop) Caution againſt Enthuſiaſm   - - - 1 | 6 6

A Sett of the foregoing Tracts, neatly bound in Twelve Volumes, may be had by any Member of the SOCIETY *for* 18 s.

As the SOCIETY, *at their annual Audit, which is generally in April, pay their Bookſeller in full to the End of the preceding Month; it is deſired that the Members will, as ſoon as they can conveniently* BEFORE THAT TIME, *remit what may be due for any Packets of Books.*

N. B. The SOCIETY have formerly taken into their Catalogue Tranſlations of ſeveral of the foregoing Tracts into the *Welch* Language, together with other Books, which, being now out of Print, are not above particularized; but if they ſhould hereafter be reprinted, they will be again added to the Catalogue.

The following BOOKS *and* TRACTS *received on the* SOCIETY's *Catalogue, are at preſent out of Print.*

DR. *Bray*'s Baptiſmal Covenant, &c. Price 1s. in Quires.
    Dr. *Mapletoft*'s Principles and Duties of the Chriſtian Religion. Price 2s. in Quires.
———— Collection of Forms of Prayer for the Uſe of Families, &c. with a plain Account of the Lord's Supper. Price 4d. in Quires.
Account of the Propagation of the Goſpel in the Eaſt. Pr. 2s. 6d. in Quires.
Turner's Spelling-Book. Price 6d. in Quires.
The Mother's Legacy to her unborn Child. Price 2½d. in Quires.
The Great Duty of Catechiſing. Price 3d. or 20s. a Hundred.
Addreſs to Grand Juries, Conſtables, and Church Wardens. Price 1½d. or 10s. a Hundred.
The Advantage of *Employing the Poor in Uſeful Labour*, and Miſchief of Idleneſs, or ill-judged Buſineſs, by Mr. *Johnſton*, of *Beverley*. Pr. 2½d. or 17s. a Hundred.

9
A Diſcourſe

A Difcourfe concerning the Laws Ecclefiaftical and Civil, made againft Hereticks by Popes, Emperors, Kings, and Councils. Price 1s.

An Impartial Examination and full Confutation of Mr. *Woolfton's* pretended Rabbi. Price 1½d. or 12s. 6d. a Hundred.

Serious Confiderations calmly propofed to the Promoters of Infidelity, *&c.* Price ½d. or 5s. a Hundred.

The great Work of our Redemption by *Jefus Corift,* &c. Price 6d.

Oath of a Conftable. Price ½d. or 3s. 6d. a Hundred.

Addrefs to Officers and Seamen in the Royal Navy. Price ½d. or 5s. a Hundred.

A Kind Caution to Watermen. Price 1d. or 5s. a Hundred.

Rev. Mr. *Blackwall's* Brief Scheme of Parochial Government. Price 2d. or 10s. a Hundred.

Conduct of the Stage confidered. Price 6d.

The Duty of Reproof. Price 1½d. or 10s. a Hundred.

Dr. *Alured Clarke's* Sermon at *Winchefter* Infirmary, *Oct.* 18, 1736. Pr. 4½d.

Archbifhop *Tillotfon* concerning the Hazard of being Saved in the Church of *Rome.* Price 3d. or 20s. a Hundred.

A Dialogue between a *Proteftant Minifter* and a *Popifh Prieft,* proving the Church of *England* to be a found Part of the Catholick Church. Price 2½d. or 18s. a Hundred.

A Proteftant's Reafons why he cannot turn Papift. Price 3d.

Account of Workhoufes for Employing and Maintaining the Poor; fetting forth their Ufefulnefs to the Public, the Rules by which they are governed, *&c.* Price 12d.

Account of the Lives and Sufferings of feveral Godly Perfons.

Dr. *Horneck's* Diffuafive from Popery.

Plaufib'e Arguments of a Romifh Prieft, Anfwered.

An Account of the Propagation of the Gofpel in the *Eaft.* Price 2s. 6d.

Leveridge's (Bifhop) Sermon on the Nature and Neceffity of Reftitution. Price 1d.

Kidder's (Bifhop) Young Man's Duty.

Mapletoft's Wifdom from abov'.

Oftervald's Grounds and Principles of the Chriftian Religion.

Monro on Chriftian Education.

Fenwick's Help for the Sincere.

Addrefs to Prifoners for Debt.

Life of *James Bonnel,* Efq.

R

Sermons at the Anniverſary Meetings of the Charity Children, from 1704 to 1728.

Sir *John Thorold*'s View of Popery.

Woodward's Riſe and Progreſs of Religious Societies.

Kenn's (Biſhop) Manual in *Welch*.

Yardley's (Archdeacon) Improvement of *Oſtervald's* Abridgment.

Burrows's Devout Pſalmodiſt.

Church Catechiſm broke, in *Welch*.

Expoſition of the Church Catechiſm, in *Engliſh* and *Welch*.

The Chriſtian Covenant, or the Baptiſmal Vow Explained.

Aſhton's Exhortation to the Holy Communion.

Prayers before, at, and after, receiving the Sacrament.

The Miracles of *Jeſus* vindicated.

Single Sermons before the Society for Propagating the Goſpel.

Drew's Admonition to diſcharged Debtors.

Franklyn's Advice to all who live upon the Sea Coaſt.

Hales's Admonition to the Drinkers of Spirituous Liquors.

Wells againſt Swearing.

Prayers for Apprentices going out of Charity Schools to Trades or Services.

Lewis's Defence of the Communion Office.

Short Refutation of the Errors of the Church of *Rome*.

Popery always the ſame.

Seaſonable Caveat againſt Popery.

White's New Preſervative againſt Popery, abridged.

S P E C I M E N S

OF THE

SEVERAL CHARACTERS

U S E D I N

Printing the Bibles,. Teftaments, and Common Prayers, difperfed by the S O C I E T Y.

BIBLE, *Pica Quarto.*

Bleffed is the man that hath not walked in the counfel of the ungodly, nor ftood in the way of finners: and hath not fat in the feat of the fcornful. But his delight is in the law of the Lord : and in his law will he excrcife himfelf day and night.

BIBLE *Brevier 8vo. and* TESTAMENT *Brevier 12mo.*

Bleffed is the man that hath not walked in the counfel of the ungodly, nor ftood in the way of finners : and hath not fat in the feat of the fcornful. But his delight is in the law of the Lord : and in his law will he exercife himfelf day and night. And he fhall be like a tree planted by the water-fide : that will bring forth his fruit in due feafon. His leaf alfo fhall not wither : and look, whatfoever he doeth it fhall profper. As for the ungodly, it is not fo with them : but they are like the wind fcattereth away from the face of the earth. Therefore the ungodly fhall not be able to ftand in the judgment : neither the finners in the congregation of the righteous. But the Lord knoweth the way of the righteous : and the way of the ungodly fhall perifh.

BIBLE *Minion, and* COMMON PRAYER *Minion,* 12mo.

Bleffed is the man that hath not walked in the counfel of the ungodly, nor ftood in the way of finners : and hath not fat in the feat of the fcornful. But his delight is in the law of the Lord : and in his law will he exercife himfelf day and night. And he fhall be like a tree planted by the water-fide : that will bring forth his fruit in due feafon. His leaf alfo fhall not wither : and look, whatfoever he doeth it fhall profper. As for the ungodly, it is not fo with them : but they are like the chaff which the wind fcattereth away from the face of the earth. Therefore the ungodly fhall not be able to ftand in the judgment : neither the finners in the congregation of the righteous. But the Lord knoweth the way of the righteous : and the way of the ungodly fhall perifh,

R 2

BIBLE

BIBLE *Nonpareil* 12mo. *Nonpareil* 24to. TESTAMENT *Nonpareil* 24to. *and* COMMON PRAYER *Nonpareil* 24to.

Bleffed is the man that hath not walked in the counfel of the ungodly, nor ftood in the way of finners: and hath not fat in the feat of the fcornful. But his delight is in the law of the Lord: and in his law will he exercife himfelf day and night. And he fhall be like a tree planted by the water-fide: that will bring forth his fruit in due feafon. His leaf alfo fhall not wither: and look, whatfoever he doeth it fhall profper. As for the ungodly, it is not fo with them: but they are like the chaff which the wind fcattereth away from the face of the earth. Therefore the ungodly fhall not be able to ftand in the judgment: neither the finners in the congregation of the righteous. But the Lord knoweth the way of the righteous: and the way of the ungodly fhall perifh.

TESTAMENT *Pica* 8vo. *and* COMMON PRAYER *Pica* 8vo.

Bleffed is the man that hath not walked in the counfel of the ungodly, nor ftood in the way of finners: and hath not fat in the feat of the fcornful. But his delight is in the law of the Lord: and in his law will he exercife himfelf day and night. And he fhall be like a tree planted by the water-fide: that will bring forth his fruit in due feafon. His leaf alfo fhall not wither: and look, whatfoever he doeth, it fhall profper.

TESTAMENT *Long Primer* 8vo.

Bleffed is the man that hath not walked in the counfel of the ungodly, nor ftood in the way of finners: and hath not fat in the feat of the fcornful. But his delight is in the law of the Lord: and in his law will he exercife himfelf day and night. And he fhall be like a tree planted by the water-fide: that will bring forth his fruit in due feafon. His leaf alfo fhall not wither: and look, whatfoever he doeth, it fhall profper.

COMMON PRAYER *Long Primer* 12mo.

Bleffed is the man that hath not walked in the counfel of the ungodly, nor ftood in the way of finners: and hath not fat in the feat of the fcornful. But his delight is in the law of the Lord: and in his law will he exercife himfelf day and night. And he fhall be like a tree planted by the water-fide: that will bring forth his fruit in due feafon. His leaf alfo fhall not wither: and look, whatfoever he doeth, it fhall profper.

COMMON PRAYER *Brevier* 12mo.

Bleffed is the man that hath not walked in the counfel of the ungodly, nor ftood in the way of finners: and hath not fat in the feat of the fcornful. But his delight is in the law of the Lord: and in his law will he exercife himfelf day and night. And he fhall be like a tree planted by the water-fide: that will bring forth his fruit in due feafon. His leaf alfo fhall not wither: and look, whatfoever he doeth it fhall profper.

Nº IV.

N.° IV.

SOME

ACCOUNT

OF THE

SOCIETY's *Proteſtant Miſſions in the*
Eaſt-Indies *for the Year* 1798.

SINCE the Publication of the laſt Account, ſeveral
Letters have been received from the Miſſionaries,
the Subſtance of which is included in the following
Particulars.

The Rev. Mr. *Swartz*, in a Letter dated at *Tanjore*,   *Tanjore.*
4th of *September*, 1797, acknowledges the Receipt of
the Secretary's Letter of this Year, together with the
uſual Stores and Preſents, Salaries and Gratuities, for
all which he aſſures the Society of their ſincere Thank-
fulneſs. He mentions that God had graciouſly preſerved their Lives and Health, and that he was ſtill
able to go through the uſual Work, though with leſs

I   Vigour

Vigour than heretofore; and that should his Life be preserved, he intended to give a full Account of the Mission, at the End of the Year, concluding with a Prayer that God would prosper the Work of their venerable Superiors.

The Rev. Mr. *Jænicke*, in a Letter dated at *Ramana-daburam*, 6th *September*, 1797, states that the building of a Chapel in that Place, (adverted to in a former Letter,) had been carried on but slowly, owing principally to the Difficulty of obtaining Materials and Labourers, and to other Circumstances which had sometimes proved disastrous enough, one of them being no less than the falling in of the Portico, not sufficiently supported. A new one, however, had been erected, and they were proceeding in the Building; the Particulars of which, when finished, he meant to describe. During his Attendance upon this Work, he had anxiously embraced all Opportunities of discharging the Duties of his Calling. The Place had often been visited by Missionaries, before the Yer 1791, and since that Year six Times by himself; yet their Stay having generally been short, the real Condition of several of the Congregations could not be discovered. From Circumstances he states, there appears to have been in that Congregation, a considerable Mixture of Members; some of them discrediting their Profession, by wicked Habits of Life, whilst others he had much Satisfaction in considering to be well-meaning Christians, walking worthy of their Calling; by which Fruit of their Labour, the Master whom they served comforted and encouraged them, not to become weary or faint. Besides his Labours on Christians, he had also had frequent Opportunities of addressing himself to Heathens; and though at that Time he had met with no immediate Success, yet he trusted in God that his Labour would not be quite in vain. About fifteen Persons in that Neighbourhood had repeatedly assured him of their Resolution to embrace the Truth, and he expected them soon

to

to come to him for Inftruction and Baptifm; which Re-
folution, if fincerely made, he was fure God would open a
Way for them to accomplifh. *Sattianaden*, with their Catechifts, and three Affiftants, had laboured in and about *Palamcotta*, as ufual, and their Labours had not been without
Succefs. He concludes with mentioning that he was in good
Health, for which he returns Thanks to God, and adds
" May he grant me Grace to ferve him, and to dif-
" charge the Duties of my Function with Vigour, and
" without Interruption; and, oh, with at leaft fome
" Succefs!"

The Rev. Mr. *Holzberg*, in a Letter dated at *Tanjore*,
8th *February*, 1798, communicates Particulars of his
fafe and happy Voyage from *England*—Mrs. *Holzberg's*
Delivery of a Child, during the Voyage—the very kind
Treatment he had experienced from Captain *Rait*—his
Arrival at *Vepery* and hofpitable Reception by Mr. *Gerické*—and his Procedure to, and Settlement at, *Tanjore*, (there to ftudy the *Malabar* Language, and fit
himfelf for the Work of the Miffion,) where he found
the venerable Mr. *Swartz* in a very declining State of
Health, but " joyful in God, and as it were living
" more in Heaven than on Earth."

The Rev. Mr. *Gerické*, in a Letter dated at *Madras*,   *Madras.*
16th *October*, 1797, ftates that both the *Englifh* and
the *Danifh* Miffionaries were well, and going on in their
refpective Labours, with Affiduity and Faithfulnefs;
but that *Ruyappen*, the Country Prieft, had died fuddenly,
whilft holding Converfation with a refpectable *Armenian*
Chriftian, to whom *Ruyappen* had been of much Service, by his Vifits and Intercourfe, as the *Armenian*
had informed Mr. *Gerické*.

Mr. *Gerické*, in another Letter, dated at *Vepery*,
13th *January*, 1798, acknowledges the Receipt of a
Letter from the Secretary, brought by the new Miffionary Mr. *Holzberg*, who had arrived at *Madras*, during
the preceding Month, with Mrs. *H.* and their Child.
He mentions that he had communicated to the other
Miffion-

Miffionaries, the Contents of the Secretary's Letter, relative to Mr. and Mrs. *Holzberg*, and that he would endeavour, as long as they fhould continue with him, to make all Things as comfortable to them, as his Circumftances and Situation would permit ; and that when the Salaries fhould arrive, he would pay him his Proportion. As foon as poffible, he intended to acccompany him, and his Family, to *Tanjore*, where he might beft learn the *Malabar* Language, and where his Affiftance would be moft wanted.

Mr. *Jænicke*, he obferves, fpent much of his Time at *Ramanad*, and *Palamcotta*—and Mr. *Swartz* had been, for three Months paft, dangeroufly ill, and was not expected to be able to preach again, his Illnefs having affected not only his bodily Strength, but alfo his Memory.

Mr. *Gericke* had received feveral Letters from Mr. *Ringeltaube*, the new Miffionary at *Calcutta*, and at his Requeft, had fent him fome *Portugueze* Books, and had informed him how a Miffion to the *Portugueze* might be beft conducted; befides which, he had fuggefted a Wifh that Mr. *Ringeltaube* would learn the *Bengal* Language, to extend the Miffion to the Natives of that Part of the Country.

He alfo mentions that he had recently had a Converfation with an Officer lately returned from *Malacca*, who had brought him Compliments from the Rev. Mr. *Clarke*, (late one of the Society's Miffionaries,) and a Requeft that Mr. *G.* would furnifh him with fome Books. The Officer informed Mr. *G.* that Mr. *Clarke* kept an *Englifh* School, and had learnt the *Malay* Language, which is the Language of that Country, and that he frequently had Conferences, on religious Subjects, with the *Malay* Chiefs. Mr. *Gericke* rejoiced at this News. Mr. *Clarke* had found a Tranflation of the whole Bible in the *Malay* Language, made by the *Dutch* Clergyman, who refided on that Coaft, and there was a Probability of his finding other Books written in

that

that Language, that might be of ufe to him: Mr. *Clarke* was at *Malacca* when the *Englifh* took it, by whom he had been engaged to officiate as Chaplain to the Garrifon.

The Stores and Prefents had arrived fafe in the Ship that conveyed Mr. *Holzberg*; and Mr. *Gerické* expreffes particular Thanks for the Supply of Books, as he had feveral Schools to provide for, there, at *Cuddalore*, at *Negapatnam*, and at the Naval Hofpital, where he officiated on *Sundays*, and vifited the Sick, Admiral *Renier* having appointed him Chaplain of the *Victorious*, and thus given him leave of Abfence to do Duty at the Hofpital.

Another Letter from Mr. *Gerické*, dated at *Tanjore*, 13th *February*, 1798, written as he obferves in Hafte, mentions that it had pleafed God to take from them their dear Father the Rev. Mr. *Swartz*, between four and five o'Clock that Evening. When Mr. *Gerické* arrived at *Tanjore* with Mr. *Holzberg*, on the fecond Inftant, he was tolerably alert, though before that Time he had been ill feveral Months: From the fecond Inftant, he grew weaker daily, which had occafioned Mr. *Gerické's* Continuance there. Mr. *Gerické* promifes to write more when he fhould hear more; and in the mean while recommends himfelf to the Society's Prayers, together with his Brethren, who with him cannot but be forely afflicted at fo melancholy, though not unexpected, an Event.

The Rev. Mr. *Pæzold*, in a Letter dated at *Vepery*, 31ft of *January*, 1798, details at Length the Labours wherein he had been occupied in the Years 1796 and 1797. The feveral Congregations of *Englifh*, *Portugueze*, and *Malabar* Chriftians, frequenting the Miffion Church at *Vepery*, had been regularly miniftered unto, by Mr. *Gerické* and himfelf, in their refpective Languages, Mr. *Pæzold* having delivered in the former of thofe Years, 86 public Difcourfes from the Pulpit, *viz.* 31 in the *Malabar*, or *Tamulian*, 29 in the *Portugueze*,

S   and

and 26 in the *Englifh* Language, each one having been com-
pofed by himfelf. On *Wednefday* and *Friday* Evenings,
they accuftomed the Scholars of the different Schools
to catechetical Inftruction, examining them in the fun-
damental Articles of the Chriftian Faith, as ftated in
the *Tamulian* and *Portugueze* Catechifms, and accordingly expounding the Ten Commandments, the Creed,
the Lord's Prayer, and the Sacraments: he laments
that but few adult Perfons frequented thefe Week-day
Evening Services. On *Wednefdays*, in the Forenoon,
the *Tamulian* Catechifts were inftructed and examined,
in the Church, to fit them for their Occupations. In
the Year 1796, he had baptized 31 Children, buried 9
Corpfes, and married 13 Couple. Previoufly to the
Adminiftration of the Lord's Supper, they gave pre-
paratory Inftructions, which ufually lafted for a Fort-
night. In the Year 1797, his Labours had been fo
fimilar to thofe of the preceding Year, that he did not
judge it needful to particularize them. To the *Dutch*
Prifoners he had preached in *Vepery* Church twice, in
the *German* Language, before their Reception of the
Lord's Supper, all of them being *Germans*. The Com-
pofition of his Pulpit Difcourfes was attended with lefs
Difficulty to him, than it had formerly been; but,
being in three different Languages, they ftill occupied
much of his Time. He goes on to enlarge on the Influence of the Climate on the human Conftitution,
particularly of *Europeans*; and the Inconvenience with
which Bufinefs, and efpecially ftudious Occupation, was
purfued in *India*: And, in Conclufion, he prays for
Bleffings on the Exertions of the Society.

Tranquebar. The Rev. the *Danifh* Miffionaries, in a Letter dated
at *Tranquebar*, 10th *February*, 1798, acknowledge
gratefully the Receipt of the annual Stores and Prefents
fent from the Society, the preceding Year, and pray
God to blefs and reward thofe, who contribute to the
Promotion of Chriftian Knowledge amongft the *Indians*,
and to the Comfort of the Labourers amongft them.
Reduced

[139]

Reduced to three Miffionaries only at *Tranquebar*, they enjoyed Health, and being cordially united together, they bore their Burden patiently, and made it, as much as poffible, fit eafy upon them. Since the Death of Mr. *Koenig*, Mr. *John* preached alternately in *Portu-gueze* and *Malabar*. The Books fent out by the Society were very acceptable, and ufeful, efpecially fince the *Englifh* Language had been introduced in the *Portugueze* Schools. Mr. *Cammerer's* Health had improved, fince his Return from *Ceylon*, fo that he could uninterruptedly perfevere in his Duty. He had recently vifited the Country Congregations and Schools, where he found that both Chriftians and Heathens excelled in Morals, and in Efteem for the Doctrines of the Gofpel, fuch as lived nearer the *Europeans*, amongft whom, it was to be lamented, that both feemed to be much on the De-creafe. They mention the Decay of Mr. *Swartz's* Faculties, and Memory in particular, and with peculiar Concern, as his Inftructions and Guidance would have been very beneficial to Mr. *Holzberg :* They refpectfully mention the Labours of Mr. *Kolhoff,* at *Tanjore,* and Mr. *Gericke's* being at that Place with Mr. *Holzberg,* and his proceeding thence to *Tiruchinapally,* to *Nega-patnam,* and aftewards to vifit them at *Tranquebar,* from whofe Converfation they always experienced Benefit. They alfo mention the Lofs they had fuf-tained, by the fudden Death of their Country Prieft *Rayoppen,* as ftated by Mr. *Gericke.*

During the preceding Year, their Baptifms had been 161, including 23 Heathens; their Burials 72, their Marriages 15, and 1209 Perfons had received the Lord's Supper. One hundred and feventy Children were in-ftructed in their Town and Country Schools, of whom more than an hundred were wholly maintained. They were then printing an Ecclefiaftical Hiftory in *Tamu-lian,* and a *Portugueze* Verfion of *Thomas à Kempis de imitatione Chrifti,* with other fmall Treatifes in both Languages.

S 2   They

They again exprefs their Gratitude to the Society for Affiftance to the Work of, the Printing Prefs, and for other benevolent Marks of liberal Attention to them; and they beg Leave to recommend themfelves to the Society's further Benevolence.

Calcutta.

The Rev. Mr. *Ringeltaube*, in a Letter dated at *Calcutta*, 27th *October*, 1797, mentions his fafe Arrival at that Place, after a Paffage of eighteen Weeks, and his very kind Reception by the Rev. Mr. *David Brown*, whom he confidered to be a truly valuable Man, and to whom accordingly he felt himfelf bound by the Tye of Chriftian Affection, as well as that of Gratitude, and to whom he meant to commit himfelf for Guidance and Advice, during his Continuance there.

Mr. *Ringeltaube*, in another Letter, dated at *Calcutta*, 10th *November*, 1797, ftates that he finds it impracticable to fubfift at *Calcutta* upon his Salary, efpecially as he had been obliged to hire a Houfe to refide in, at a confiderable Expence, and to provide Servants; and intimates that if fome additional Allowance be not made, nothing will remain for him to do but to think of an honourable Retreat.

The *Eaft India* Miffion Committee, taking into Confideration the whole of the Particulars communicated by Mr. *Ringeltaube*, and being likewife informed by *Charles Grant*, Efq; that he had received Letters from *Calcutta*, in which Mr. *R.* was very honourably mentioned, agreed in Opinion, and the General Board concurred in the fame, that an Addition of £.50 *per Annum*, fhould be made to Mr. *Ringeltaube's* Salary, till fuch Time as he fhould be put into Poffeffion of the Apartments, erected for the Ufe of a Miffionary, over the School Houfe, attached to the Miffion Church, and that immediate Endeavours fhould be ufed to procure for him the Poffeffion of thofe Apartments. Letters to this Effect were therefore tranfmitted to *Calcutta*; in which it was alfo intimated to Mr. *R.* that teaching of a School was Part of the original Plan of the *Cal-*

I

cutta Miffion, and that by the Superintendance of the
School, he might derive a comfortable Addition to his
Income.

THE ufual Stores and Prefents of Books, Stationary,
and other Articles of Accommodation, together with
the Remittances, including a Gratuity of £ 50 to each
of the Miffionaries, in addition to their Salaries, have
been fent out this Year, through the continued Favor
of the Honorable *Eaft India* Company ; to whom the
SOCIETY thus publicly return their HEARTY THANKS.

MISSION

MISSION

TO THE

SCILLY ISLANDS.

IT appearing to the Committee appointed for regu-
lating the Miſſion to the *Scilly Iſlands*, that they
would better underſtand the Circumſtances of that
Miſſion, and be better enabled to conduct its Concerns,
if ſome Member, deputed by the Society, were to viſit
the Iſlands, they ſuggeſted to the Board their Wiſh that
the Rev. Dr. *Gaſkin*, the Society's Secretary, might be
requeſted to undertake ſuch Viſitation, ſhould it be
found agreeable and convenient to him, in order to
collect full Information on various Particulars of Importance to the Welfare of the Miſſion. Accordingly,
after maturely conſidering the Suggeſtion, the Board
concurred in the Opinion that ſuch a Meaſure would be
attended with beneficial Effects. It being therefore
propoſed to the Rev. the Secretary, he readily acceded
to the Propoſal ; and having obtained the Concurrence
of the Lord Biſhop of *Exeter*, of whoſe Dioceſe the
Iſlands of *Scilly* make a Part, and a very obliging Pro-
miſe from the Lords of the Admiralty, of a Paſſage on
Board of one of his Majeſty's Veſſels from *Penzance* to
the Iſlands, he ſat out on his Journey to the Weſt of
England at the latter End of *July*, 1798, and, under
the

9

the Protection and Blessing of God, happily accomplished the Ends he had in View. During his Absence from Town, he kept a Diary, and entered in it every material Circumstance that occurred, and which he noticed, as connected with the Society's Concerns in general, and with the Mission to the *Scilly Islands* in particular. From this Journal, which was submitted to the Inspection of the Committee, and from the Doctor's additional Reports in Reply to their Enquiries, the Committee got furnished with a large Measure of Information relative to the Islands, and the Society's Concerns in them; and accordingly they made an ample and very satisfactory Report thereof to the Board. They stated to the Board, that " the Abundance and Value " of the Information they had acquired through his " judicious and zealous Endeavours, fully evinced the " Necessity of the Measure, and would be always most " advantageous to the Committee, in its future Regula- " tion of the Missions." The Committee went on to observe, that " it required nothing less than the Pru- " dence, Discretion, and Christian Charity, which " distinguish his Character, to accomplish the Objects " of this Visitation, which could never have been at- " tained, unless the State of the Mission had been sub- " jected to the ocular Inspection of some Person so " eminently qualified.

" By Direction of the Lords of the Admiralty, to " Commodore Sir *Edward Pellew*, Bart. the Secretary " was conveyed from *Penzance* to *Scilly*, and back " again, on board his Majesty's Gun Brig *Assault*; " where he experienced every obliging Attention from " the Commander, Lieutenant *Hicks*; and in *Scilly*; " he was received in the most attentive and courteous " Manner, by the Commandant, Major *Bowen*, at " *Star* Castle, and with very great Respect by the " Islanders in general.

" During his Abode among them, he attended divine " Service, and preached in all the Churches of the " several Islands.

" The

" The Committee, previous to Dr. *Gaſkin's* De-
" parture, ſubmitted to him certain Points of Infor-
" mation, not by Way of Inſtruction, but for the Sake
" of Aſſiſtance to his Memory; and, on every one of
" theſe Points, the Committee received the moſt per-
" fect Satisfaction.

" The firſt Point of Enquiry, which engaged the
" Attention of the Committee, was the general Cha-
" racter of the Inhabitants ; and they were reported to
" them to be an inoffenſive well-diſpoſed People, de-
" firous of Inſtruction, reſpectfully attached to their
" Miniſters, and grateful to the Society for the Exer-
" tions it has uſed towards their Improvement in reli-
" gious Knowledge. There was found only one unau-
" thorized Teacher on the Iſlands, and he of the *Weſleyan*
" Sect, and there did not appear either in him, or
" among his Followers, any Enmity to the Church of
" *England*, or any Diſaffection to Government. The
" Advantages derived to the Iſlanders from the Im-
" provements in the State of the Miſſion are incalcu-
" lable ; and they muſt daily increaſe, not only from
" the Exertions of the Miſſionaries, but from the Diſ-
" poſition, with which their Endeavours are generally
" received.

" No Encouragement, the Committee apprehends,
" can be too great, to the Perſeverance of the Miſſi-
" onaries, in the Diſcharge of their ſacred Duties.
" Situated as they are, where the common Comforts of
" Life are ſparingly to be found, the Committee, and
" the Board at large wiſh to ſupply them with whatever
" of this Sort may be deemed expedient. One prin-
" cipal Object, relative to this Point, was the building
" of the ſenior Miſſionary's Houſe. It has been judged
" expedient to relinquiſh a Piece of Land, originally
" deſtined for this Purpoſe, on Account of ſome In-
" conveniencies ariſing from the preſent Tenures, and
" the Neceſſity which would have exiſted of diſpoſſeſſing
" certain Perſons, who are ſtrongly attached to that
" Spot.

" Spot. Other Pieces of Land, however, have been
" found, one of which will be the Site of the Miſſion-
" ary's Houſe, the other at no inconvenient Diſtance is
" a Portion of arable and Paſture Land, conſiſting of
" three or four Acres, which is indiſpenſably neceſſary
" for the Miſſionary at *Treſco*;" and his Grace the
Lord Proprietor has executed a Leaſe of theſe Lands,
in Truſt for the Society, at the ſmall Rent of ſixteen
Shillings *per Annum*; ſo that the Building may now be
commenced.

" Another Point of Enquiry was into the State of the
" Places of public Worſhip, in the Off Iſlands. The
" Church of *Treſco* was found to be old and ſmall,
" only 30 Feet long by 15 broad, but having Galleries
" at one End, and on one Side, incapable neverthelefs
" of containing the Inhabitants. To remedy this De-
" fect, the Committee propoſed," and the Society have
agreed " to allow the Sum of £.25 to the Inhabitants, in
" Aid of repairing and enlarging the Church, by the
" Addition of a Chancel to be 15 Feet long, and 12 in
" Breadth. The Church of *Brehar*, built in 1743, is
" 24 Feet in Length, by 15 in Breadth; and though
" it has no Gallery, is competent to hold not only the
" Inhabitants of *Brehar*, but thoſe alſo of the adjacent
" Iſland of *Sampſon*. The Church of St. *Martin's* is
" in Length 31 Feet 4 Inches, and in Breadth 15 Feet
" 4 Inches, and is ſpacious enough to contain the In-
" habitants. In this Church only were found the
" Commandments inſcribed on Boards." It is but in
indifferent Repair, and the Society have thought fit,
on the Suggeſtion of the Committee, to grant £.5 to
the Inhabitants, if they will undertake to repair it com-
pletely.

" The Church of St. *Agnes* was built in 1685, and
" was lengthened in 1795, by the Inhabitants at their
" own Expence. It is very nearly 38 Feet long, and
" 15 in Breadth. It is in good Repair, and has a Gal-
" lery; but neither here, nor in any of the Off-Iſland
T   " Churches

" Churches is there a Pulpit," the Sermon being
preached in the Reading-Defk.
" The Society's Schools have always been an Object
" of the Committee's particular Attention. In the
" Directions given to the Miffionaries, previous to
" their Departure, every Exertion was made to imprefs
" ftrongly upon their Minds the Duty of watching
" over them with unremitted Attention ; and when this
" Vifitation was undertaken by Dr. *Gafkin*, he expreffed
" his Solicitude refpecting this moft important Con-
" cern, and proved by the Manner of his Inveftigation
" into the State of the Schools, his Zeal for the In-
" terefts of true Religion, the Salvation of Souls, and
" the Advantage of the rifing Generation. Some of
" the Schools were found to be in a better State, than
" either he, or the Committee had Reafon to expect ;"
but certain Improvements were fuggefted by the Committee.

The School at *Trefco* was then under the Care of the
Widow *Pender*, who was 70 Years of Age. She taught
all the Children of that Ifland, for the fmall Confideration of £.3 a Year. Dr. *Gafkin*, on Examination
found that the Children read tolerably, and anfwered
well in the Church Catechifm. From this good Woman's advanced Age and Infirmities, who had taught
the Grandfathers and Grandmothers of thofe then under
her Care, fhe could fcarcely be able to continue much
longer in the Bufinefs of School-teaching. The Society therefore have granted her an Annuity of £.5
during the Remainder of her Life, and directed that
£.7 *per Annum* fhould in future be allowed as a Salary
for a good Mafter or Miftrefs of this School, as foon
as fuch an one fhould be procured by the Miffionary.

At *Brehar* was a good School Miftrefs, who for a
Salary of £1. 10s. *per Annum*, had taught all the Children, about 12 or 15 in Number. This Perfon was
very favourably reported of by the Miffionary ; and her
Salary has been augmented to £.3 a Year.

A School

A School Houſe at St. *Martin's* had been built by
the Inhabitants. The Maſter was *James Nance*, who,
for £.3 a Year, had taught 15 Children, on the Society's
Account. His Income was made £.9 a Year, by teaching Children, whoſe Parents paid him. On the Recommendation of the Committee, the Society have
allowed *James Nance* £.10 *per Annum*, on Condition
that he ſhall teach all Children, that ſhall be appointed
by the Miſſionary; becauſe in that State of the School,
the Miſſionary could not have the proper Management
of it, and was precluded from extending its Benefits to
more than 15 Children, although there were many more
in Want of Inſtruction. This School was found to be
well taught.

All the Children in the Iſland of St. *Agnes*, were
taught by the Widow *Mary Hicks*, for £.3 *per Annum*.
This School was very indifferently taught, the Miſtreſs
being 74 Years of Age, and grown incapable of her
Buſineſs. The £.3 *per Annum* will be continued to her,
during the Remainder of her Life ; and an Allowance
in future of £.5 a Year to a new Maſter, or Miſtreſs,
if one well qualified can be found by the Miſſionary.

At *Sampſon*, the Miſtreſs was the Widow *Webber*,
whoſe Salary was £.1 10s. *per Annum*, and who had
never had more than 6 or 7 Children under her Care.
With this School Miſtreſs, the Miſſionary was diſſatis-
fied; therefore no Augmentation has been granted to
her ; but, in Caſe a new one properly qualified ſhould
be found, the Salary will be advanced to £.3 *per Annum*.

In St. *Mary's* Iſland, there are two Schools, one in
Heugh Town, the other in the Country. That in the
Town, was taught by the Widow *Scaddon*. She had been
12 Years Miſtreſs, and taught 24 Children for the Society, for £.5 *per Annum*. She alſo had in her School
other Children, whoſe Parents paid for their Inſtruction.
She was found to be a Woman of good Character, and
a very good Teacher. The Society therefore have augmented her Salary to £.8 *per Annum* for teaching their

T 2   Children.

Children. Mrs. *M'Farlane*, an aged and bedridden Woman, had long been the Miftrefs of the Country School,
which was then taught by her Daughter ; the Society's
Children being 24 in Number, and the Salary £.5 a
Year, which has been encreafed to £.8.

It having been judged expedient, by the Committee,
and by the General Board, that a fmall Collection of
theological Books fhould be fent for the Ufe of each
Miffionary, and his Succeffors, this Meafure has been
adopted. The Sum of £.15 for each Collection has
been granted, and the Committee have felected fuch
Books as to them feemed moft ufeful to the Miffionaries; befides which, a fuitable Packet of other Books
has been ordered for Diftribution amongft the Iflanders.

The Board, perfectly fatisfied with the Declaration
of the Committee, that they had received from the
Reverend the Secretary, " the moft ample Information,
" which could poffibly be defired on every Point, that
" was an Object of Enquiry, recommended to him by
" the Committee ;" (and the Committee having alfo
fignified to the Board " their higheft Approbation of
" his whole Conduct, both in public and private Con-
" cerns, during his Vifitation of the *Scilly* Iflands,")
granted the Sum of £.100 to defray the Expences of
his Journey, and Vifitation, and unanimoufly voted
him THEIR THANKS.

No. V.

N° V.

An A B S T R A C T of the Proceedings of the S o c i e t y *for Promoting Chriſtian Knowledge*, for the Year 1798.

THE *Subſcribing* and *Correſponding* Members of the Society in *Great-Britain* and Foreign Parts, are now upwards of 1900, of which Number, 122 Subſcribing Members, were choſen ſince the Publication of the laſt Account; and 32 Ladies have likewiſe been admitted on the Liſt of annual Subſcribers.

B o o k s *and* P a p e r s *preſented to the* S o c i e t y.

2 Copies of " The Political and Moral Conſequences reſulting, reſpectively, from Religious Education and its Reverſe, deduced from Hiſtory and Example," by the Dean of *Middleham*; being a Preſent from the Author.

6 Copies of " A Sermon preached before the Military Aſſociation of *Chriſt Church, Surry*," by the Rev. *Thomas Ackland*, M.A. Rector of tha Pariſh; being a Preſent from the Author.

18 Copies of " A Sermon, preached before the *Bridge, Candlewick*, and *Dowgate* Wards, Military Aſſociations," by the Rev. *William Vincent*, D.D. Sub-Almoner to his Majeſty; being a Preſent from the Author.

26

4   18 Copies

Books, &c. *Continued.*

26 Brought over.
18 Copies of " A Sermon, preached before the Military Affociation of *Stoke-Newington*," by the Rev. *George Gafkin*, D.D. being a Prefent from the Author.

6 Copies of a Vifitation Sermon, " Entitled a Difpaffionate Enquiry into the Probable Caufes and Confequences of Enthufiafm," by the Rev. *Jofeph Eyre*, M.A. Vicar of St.. *Giles's, Reading* ; being a Prefent from the Author.

25 Copies of the Second Edition of " A Sermon on the 109th Pfalm," by the Rev. *Samuel Partridge*, M.A. Vicar of *Bofton*, *Lincolnfhire* ; being a Prefent from the Author.

18 Copies of " A Sermon preached before the Houfe of Lords, on *Wednefday*, *February* 27, 1799," by the Right Rev. *Shute*, Lord Bifhop of *Durham* ; being a Prefent from the Author.

50 Copies of a Tract entitled, " An Exhortation to receive the Holy Sacrament, extracted from the Pious Country Parifhioner ;" being a Prefent from a Perfon unknown.

25 Copies of " A Sermon preached before the Society for the Propagation of the Gofpel in Foreign Parts," by the Right Rev. *Spencer*, Lord Bifhop of *Peterborough* ; being a Prefent from that Society.

2 Copies of " Sermons preached before the Right Hon. *Paul Le Mefurier*, (in 1794,) and the Right Hon. *Brook Watfon*, (in 1797,) Lord Mayors of *London*," by the Rev. *Geo. S. Townley*, M.A. Chaplain to their Lordfhips.

———
170 Total.

Books

BOOKS *and* PAPERS *Bought or Printed by Order of the* SOCIETY.

3500 Copies of the Rev. Dr. *John Law*'s Sermon preached at the Anniverfary Meeting, &c.
3500 Copies of the Origin and Defigns of the Society.
7500 —— Pfalms for the Ufe of the Charity Children.
563 Copies of Directions for the devout Ufe of the Common-Prayer, in *Octavo*.
10077 Ditto, *Duodecimo*.
Copies of Forms of Prayer to be ufed at Sea.
Quarto Sheets on Pfalmody.

25140 Total

1018 PACKETS *fent* to Subfcribing and Correfponding Members; confifting of

Bibles, — — — 5572
New Teftaments and Pfalters, — — 7521
Common Prayers, — — — 10658
Other Bound Books, — — — 14395
Small Tracts—Some in Half Binding—Others Stitched, — — — } 82559

In all 120705

RECEIPTS and PAYMENTS of the
from 22 March 1798,

RECEIPTS.

	£.	s.	d.
BALANCE due to the Society, as ſtated laſt Audit	890	15	6
Benefactions and Legacies to the General Deſigns of the Society - - - -	401	18	6
Subſcriptions from the Members of the Society -	1734	7	0
Received of the Members for Packets -	1083	3	2
Received of the Members, Arrears for Packets -	1132	17	8
Dividends of Funds for the General Deſigns .	1297	14	6
Ditto received at the Accountant-General's Office	2818	10	6
Dividends of Funds to the *Manks* Impreſſion -	42	0	0
Dividends and Benefactions towards the Support of a Miſſion and Schools in the Iſlands of *Scilly* -	26	1	6
Dividends of £. 100 in Truſt for a Sacrament on Holy-days at *Bow* Church - -	3	0	0
Dividends and Rent for Mr. *Belke's* Charity -	53	18	0
Intereſt on Mr. *Scott's* Legacy - - -	5	12	0
Four Years Rent of the *Willingham* Eſtate, due Lady Day, 1797 - - -	86	13	4
Received on Account of the late Rev. Mr. *Scott's* Legacy, by the Rev. Mr. *Gee* -	144	1	6
Balance due to the Treaſurers - -	185	0	8
By Omiſſion, in the Treaſurer's Book, of an Entry of a Payment to the Printer, on Account	60	0	0

$$£. \quad 9965 \quad 13 \quad 10$$

Society *for Promoting Christian Knowledge,* *to* 29 March, 1799.

P A Y M E N T S.	£.	s.	d.
PAID Meſſrs. *Rivington's* for Books and Packets ſent to the Members - - -	436	13	5
Paid Ditto on Account of Stores - -	924	17	9
Paper and Printing for the Anniverſary Sermon, with an Account of the Society and other Books	323	13	8
Expences of the Anniverſary Meeting of the Charity-Children, *June* 1, 1798 - -	50	0	0
Salaries and Preſents to the *Engliſh* and *Daniſh* Miſſionaries in the *Eaſt-Indies*; Books, &c.	1185	15	11
Expences on Account of the *Scilly* Miſſion -	439	13	1
Boxes for Packing, Poſtage, Stationary Wares, Houſe Repairs, diſperſing the Anniverſary Sermon, Stamps for Receipts, Inſurance, and other incidental Expences - - -	197	11	3
Land-Tax, Pariſh Dues, and Salaries to the Officers of the Society, being five Quarterly Payments to *Lady Day*, 1799 - -	768	18	6
Paid on Account of Mr. *Belke's* Charity for Books	40	13	7
Donation to the Rev. Mr. *Triebner*, late Miſſionary from the Society, to *Ebenezer* in *Georgia* -	100	0	0
Annuity to Ditto - - - -	50	0	0
Paid towards the Morning Sacrament at *Bow* Church for two Years - - -	3	0	0
Paid on Account of the new Impreſſion of the *Welſh* Bible - - - -	1440	2	0
Law Expences - - - -	44	9	8
	£. 9965	13	10

N. B. Arrears remaining due, on Ac-
count of Subſcription, about ⎰ 600 0 0
Arrears for Books 1798, and prior   778 6 8
Ditto at the Audit 1799 -   1364 16 7

Total Amount of theſe Arrears £. 2143 3 3

U

Cafual BENEFACTIONS and LEGACIES
to the General Defigns *of the* SOCIETY, *from*
22ᵈ March 1798, *to the* 29ᵗʰ March, 1799.

A.

			£.	s.	d.
1798 *May* 8.	MRS. *ADDERLEY*, at Adm.		1	1	0
	Adam Afkew, Efq;	-	1	1	0
1799 *Jan.* 29.	*J. P. Anderdon*, Efq; at Adm.		3	3	0
Mar. 12.	Mrs. R. *Afheton*, at Admiffion		1	1	0
	John Ackland, Efq; at Admiffion		1	1	0
	Mrs. *Lydia Amphlet*, at Admiffion		1	1	0

B.

1798 *May* 8.	Lady *Bagot*	-	-	1	1	0
	R. *Burdon*, Efq; at Admiffion			1	1	0
June 12.	Hon. Mrs. *Barrington*, at Admiffion		1	1	0
	J. Bacon, Efq;	-		2	2	0
Sept. 25.	*W. Brereton*, Efq; at Admiffion		1	1	0
	Rev. *H. Budd*, at Admiffion		1	1	0
	Mrs. *E. Bentham*	-		1	1	0
	T. Bond, Efq; at Admiffion		1	1	0

Carried over - 17 17 0

			£.	s.	d.
	Brought over		17	17	0
1799 Jan. 8.	Rev. James Bolton, at Admiffion		1	1	0
Mar. 12.	Lady Bagot - - -		1	1	0
	Rev. J. H. Bromley, at Admiffion		1	1	0
	R. W. Blencowe, Efq; at Admiffion		1	1	0
29.	Rev. T. Barnard, at Admiffion.		1	1	0

C.

		£.	s.	d.
1798 May 8.	Rev. Colfton Carr, at Admiffion	1	1	0
23.	Rev. Dr. Charles Cooper, at Adm.	2	2	0
Sept. 25.	Mr. Anthony Clarke, at Admiffion	1	1	0
	Rev. H. Campbell, at Admiffion	1	1	0
	Rev. G. T. Carwithen, at Adm.	1	1	0
	Rev. F. Capper, at Admiffion	1	1	0
	Rev. T. Coney, at Admiffion	1	1	0
	Rev. A. J. Crefpin, at Admiffion	1	1	0
Nov. 6.	Rev. —— Camplin, at Admiffion	1	1	0
	Rev. James Cope, at Admiffion	1	1	0
1799 Jan. 8.	Mrs. Jane Cotton, at Admiffion	1	1	0
	Mrs. F. Clarke, at Admiffion	2	2	0
29.	G. Cherry, Efq; at Admiffion	1	1	0
Mar. 12.	Right Hon. Lord Cremorne, at Adm.	2	2	0
29.	Rev. J. Cooke, at Admiffion	1	1	0

D.

		£.	s.	d.
1798 May 23.	Rev. R. Davies, at Admiffion	1	1	0
Sept. 25.	Rev. W. Dickens, at Admiffion	1	1	0
	Jeremiah Dyfon, Efq; at Admiffion	1	1	0
	Rev. P. S. Dod, at Admiffion	1	1	0
1799 Jan. 29.	Rev. J. Dennis, at Admiffion	1	1	0

E.

		£.	s.	d.
1799 Jan. 5.	G. Edwards, Efq; at Admiffion	1	1	0

	£.	s.	d.
Carried over -	48	0	0

	£.	s.	d.
Brought over	48	6	o

F.

	£.	s.	d.
1798 *June* 12. Mrs. *J. Floyer*, at Admiſſion	1	1	o
Sept. 25. Miſs *A. Finch*, at Admiſſion	1	1	o
Nov. 6. Rev. *John Fennell*, at Admiſſion	1	1	o
1799 *Jan.* 29. Rev. *G. S. Faber*, at Admiſſion	1	1	o
Mar. 12. Rev. *W. J. French*, at Admiſſion	1	1	o

G.

	£.	s.	d.
1798 *May* 8. Mrs. *Mary Gratwicke*, at Admiſſion	3	3	o
Mr. *W. R. Gilbert*, at Admiſſion	1	1	o
Rev. *T. F. Gower*, at Admiſſion	1	1	o
Sept. 25. Rev. *C. Green*, at Admiſſion	1	1	o
E. C. Gregory, Eſq; at Admiſſion	1	1	o
Rev. *P. Guillebaud*, at Admiſſion	1	1	o
Rev. *J. Garnet*, at Admiſſion	1	1	o
1799 *Jan.* 8. Mr. *W. R. Gilbert* - -	1	1	o
Mar. 12. Mr. *J. Griffin*, at Admiſſion	1	1	o

H.

	£.	s.	d.
1798 *May* 8. *Quarles Harris*, Eſq; at Admiſſion	2	o	o
June 12. Lady *Eliz. Finch Hatton*, at Adm.	1	1	o
Mrs. *S. Hayter*, at Admiſſion	1	1	o
Miſs *Hadſley*, at Admiſſion	1	1	o
Miſs *M. Hadſley*, at Admiſſion	1	1	o
Sept. 25. *G. Hibbert*, Eſq; at Admiſſion	1	1	o
Nov. 6. *H. Hall*, D.C.L. at Admiſſion	1	1	o
1799 *Jan.* 29. Rev. *R. Hankinſon*, at Admiſſion	1	1	o
Mar. 12. Mrs. *Hacker*, at Admiſſion	1	1	o
H. Hudſon, Eſq; at Admiſſion	1	1	o
Rev. *D. Hollingbury*, at Admiſſion	2	2	o

Carried over -	78	13	o

[157]

	£.	s.	d.
Brought over -	78	13	0

J.

	£.	s.	d.
1798 *June* 12. *J. C. Jervoice*, Efq; at Admiffion	5	5	0

K.

	£.	s.	d.
1798 *Sept.* 25. Rev. Mr. *Kendall* - -	1	1	0
1799 *Jan.* 29. *Nathaniel Kemp*, Efq; -	1	1	0

L.

	£.	s.	d.
1798 *May* 8. *Samuel Lichiggery*, Efq; at Adm.	1	1	0
Legacy of Mrs. *S. Long*, Stamp deducted - -	188	0	0
June 12. Hon. and Rev. Mr. *Lindfey*, at Admiffion - -	1	1	0
A Lady in *Norfolk* - -	1	1	0
1799 *Jan.* 29. Rev. *B. Lawrence*, at Admiffion	1	1	0
A Lady, by the Rev. Mr. *Farrer*	1	1	0
Mar. 29. Rev. *C. Lucas*, at Admiffion -	1	1	0

M.

	£.	s.	d.
1798 *May* 8. Lady *Myddelton*, at Admiffion	3	3	0
15. Rev. *J. Morres*, at Admiffion	1	1	0
23. Hon. Mrs. *Marfham*, at Admiffion	2	2	0
June 12. Rev. *Giles Meech*, at Admiffion	1	1	0
Sept. 25. Mr. *J. W Middelton*, at Admiffion	1	1	0
Nov. 6. Rev. *S. Marfher*, at Admiffion	1	1	0
1799 *Mar.* 12. Rev. *P. C. Myddelton*, at Admiffion	1	1	0
C. T. Morgan, Efq; at Admiffion	1	1	0
W. Manning, Efq; at Admiffion	2	2	0
J. May, Efq; at Admiffion -	1	1	0
A Member - - -	20	0	0
Carried over -	315	0	0

				£.	s.	d.
		Brought over		315	0	0
1799	*Mar.* 12.	Mr. *John Moser*, at Admiffion		1	1	0
	29.	Rev. *T. Mears*, at Admiffion		1	1	0

N.

1798	*June* 12.	*Jofiah Nottidge*, Efq;	-	1	1	0
	Sept. 25.	*Jofiah Nottidge*, Efq; at Admiffion		1	1	0
1799	*Jan.* 8.	Rev. *Thomas Neate*, at Admiffion		1	1	0

O.

1799	*Jan.* 8.	Lady *H. Ofborne*, at Admiffion		1	1	0

P.

1798	*May* 8.	Mrs. *Dorothy Parker*, at Adm.		1	1	0
		Mr. *Nathaniel Planner*, at Adm.		1	1	0
	23.	*J. Puget*, Efq; at Admiffion		1	1	0
		Mrs. *Puget*, at Admiffion	-	1	1	0
		Mrs. *M. Paulett*, at Admiffion		1	1	0
	Sept. 25.	Rev. *T. Pennington*, at Admiffion		1	1	0
		Rev. *C. Poole*, at Admiffion	-	1	1	0
	Nov. 6.	Rev. *J. Prowett*, at Admiffion		1	1	0
1799	*Jan.* 8.	Lady *Parkyns*, at Admiffion	-	2	2	0

R.

1798	*May* 8.	Rev. *Thomas Robinfon*	-	0	10	6
		Mifs *Rolle*, at Admiffion	-	1	1	0
	Sept. 23.	Rev. *L. Richmond*, at Admiffion		1	1	0
		Mifs *M. Rooke*, at Admiffion	-	1	1	0
1799	*Jan.* 8.	Rev. *W. Rofe*, at Admiffion	-	2	2	0
		Rev. *T. C. Rudftone*, at Adm.		2	2	0

		Carried over	-	339	13	6

			£.	s.	d.
		Brought over	359	13	6
1799	Mar. 12.	Mr. J. Rutter, at Admiffion -	1	1	o
		Mrs. A. Ridfdale, at Admiffion -	1	1	o
	29.	Rev. C. Richards, at Admiffion	1	1	o
		Rev. T. Robinfon, at Admiffion	1	1	o

S.

1798	May 8.	Rev. J. Stubbs, at Admiffion -	1	1	o
		Rev. T. H. Spurrier, at Adm.	1	1	o
	Nov. 6.	Rev. T. Salmon, at Admiffion	1	1	o
1799	Jan. 8.	C. S. Strong, Efq; at Admiffion	1	1	o
		Rev. Dr. Sumner, at Admiffion	1	1	o
	29.	Rev. R. Stopford, at Admiffion	1	1	o
	Mar. 12.	J. Sargeant, Efq; at Admiffion	1	1	o
		Mrs. Simeon, at Admiffion -	2	2	o

T.

1798	Sept. 25.	Rev. R. Tillard, at Admiffion	1	1	o
		Rev. J. Tomlin, at Admiffion	1	1	o
1799	Jan. 29.	Rev. W. Tate, at Admiffion -	1	1	o
	Mar. 12.	Rev. G. A. Thomas, at Admiffion	2	2	o
	29.	Rev. Jeremiah Trift, at Admiffion	1	1	o
		Colonel Thornton, at Admiffion	1	1	o

U.

1798	June 12.	A Lady unknown, by Mr. Tilbury	15	o	o
1799	Jan. 29.	Mrs. Udney - - -	1	1	o

V.

1798	Nov. 8.	Mifs Vanfittart, at Admiffion	2	2	o
1799	Jan. 8.	Hon. G. Villars, at Admiffion	1	1	o

| | Carried over - | 379 | 17 | 6 |

			£.	s.	a.
	Brought over		379	17	6
1799 *Jan.* 29.	Rev. *W. Vincent*, at Admiſſion		1	1	0
Mar. 12.	Rev. *P. Vaillant*, at Admiſſion		1	1	0

W.

			£.	s.	a.
1798 *May* 8.	Mrs. *Jane Worthington*, at Adm.		1	1	0
	Mrs. *Wilſon* - - -		2	2	0
23.	Rev. *W. B. Whitfeld*, at Admiſſion		1	1	0
June 12.	Rev. Mr. *Wrangham*, at Admiſſion		1	1	0
	Rev. *J. Watſon*, at Admiſſion		1	1	0
	Rev. *J. Williams*, at Admiſſion		1	1	0
Sept. 25.	Rev. *J. Williams*, at Admiſſion		1	1	0
	Mr. *G. Walker*, at Admiſſion -		2	2	0
	Rev. *J. Whitaker*, at Admiſſion		1	1	0
	Rev. *W. Wyatt*, at Admiſſion -		1	1	0
1799 *Jan.* 8.	Rev. *George Whitmore*, at Adm.		1	1	0
	Rev. *Thomas Whateley*, at Adm.		1	0	0
Mar. 12.	*W. Wickham*, Eſq; at Admiſſion		2	2	0
	Mrs. *Wilſon* -- - -		2	2	0

Y.

			£.	s.	a.
1799 *Mar.* 12.	Rev. *R. Yates*, at Admiſſion -		1	1	0

Total Benefactions and Legacies £. 401 18 6

BENE-

DIVIDENDS *to the Impreffion of the* HOLY BIBLE, *and other Religious Books, in the Vulgar Language of the* Iſle of Mann, *from* 22ᵈ March, 1798, *to the Audit,* 29ᵗʰ March, 1799.

		£.	s.	d.
1799 *Mar.* 22. Twelve Months Dividend on £. 1100 New *South Sea* Annuities, due at *Chriſtmas* 1798 - -		33	o	o
Twelve Months Dividends on £. 300 Old *South Sea* Annuities, due at *Michaelmas* 1798		9	o	o
	£.	42	o	o

BENEFACTIONS *and* DIVIDENDS *to the Eſtabliſhment of a Miſſion in the* Scilly Iſlands, *from the Audit* 22ᵈ March, 1798, *to the Audit* 29ᵗʰ March, 1799.

	£.	s.	d.
1799 *Mar.* 22. Twelve Months Dividend on £.750 N.S.S.A. due at *Chriſt-mas* 1798 - - - -	22	10	o
Twelve Months Dividend on £. 119 4s. 3 per Cent. due at *Chriſt-mas* 1798, being the joint Bene-faction of the late Rev. *T. Bentham,* and Mrs. *Philippa Bentham,* of *Stockport, Cheſhire* -	3	11	6
£.	26	1	6

The SOCIETY hereby defire all the foregoing Benefactors to their feveral Defigns to accept of their moſt hearty Thanks.

X   The

The Names of the Missionaries, employed by the SOCIETY, with the certain Annual * Salaries paid to them respectively.

In the EAST-INDIES.

£.

THE Reverend *Christian William Gericke*, Missionary at *Madras* - - } 50

The Rev. *Christian Pohle*, Missionary at *Tirutshinapally* 50

The Reverend *Joseph Daniel Jænicke*, Missionary at *Palamcotta* - - - - } 50

The Reverend *John Caspar Kolboff*, Missionary at *Tanjore* - - - - } 50

The Reverend *Charles William Pæzold*, Missionary at *Madras* - - - - - } 50

The Reverend *William Toby Ringeltaube*, Missionary at *Calcutta* - - - - } 50

The Reverend *Immanuel Gottfried Holzberg*, Missionary at *Madras* - - - } 50

In the ISLANDS OF SCILLY.

The Reverend *David Evans*, M. A. Missionary at *Tresco* - - - - } 100

The Rev. *Frederick Croker*, B. A. Missionary at *St. Agnes* - - - - } 100

* Besides a Gratuity of £. 50 to each of the Missionaries in *India*.

The

The proper FORM by which any Benefaction may be given to the Defigns of the Society, to prevent any Doubt or Miſtake, is as follows :

I TE M, *I* A. B. *do hereby give and bequeath unto* C. D. *of* and E. F. *of the Sum of*
to be raiſed and paid by and out of all my ready Money, Plate, Goods, and Perſonal Effecis, which by Law I may, or can charge with the Payment of the ſame, (and not out of any Part of my Lands, Tenements, or Hereditaments) upon Truſt, and to the Intent that they, or either of them, do pay the ſame to the Treaſurer or Treaſurers for the Time being, of a Voluntary Society, commonly called or known by the Name of, THE SOCIETY FOR PROMOTING CHRISTIAN KNOWLEDGE, *which firſt met about the latter End of the Year* 1698 ; *and now do, or lately did, hold their Weekly Meetings at their Houſe in* Bartlett's Buildings, Holborn : *Which ſaid Sum of*
I deſire may be applied towards carrying on the Charitable Deſigns of the ſaid Society.

N. B. The Variation in this Form of a LEGACY from that formerly printed, is made neceſſary, on Account of ſome unhappy Miſtakes in Wills ; by which ſome Legacies have been loſt to the Society, and the good Intentions of the Teſtators have been entirely defeated ; becauſe the Sums bequeathed to the Society have been ordered to be raiſed, or paid out of Lands, or real Eſtates, which is not now permitted by Law.

₊ If the Benefactor is pleaſed to reſtrain his Charity to any particular Branch of the SOCIETY's Deſigns, he may add, either *in Great-Britain,* the *Eaſt-Indies,* the *Scilly* Iſlands, the *Manks,* or *Welch* Impreſſion of the Holy Scriptures.

A LIST

A

L I S T

OF THE

BISHOPS, DEANS, &c.

Who have Preached at the

Yearly Meeting of the CHILDREN Educated in the CHARITY SCHOOLS, in and about the Cities of *London* and *Weſtminſter*.

Anno
1704   THE Reverend Dr. *Willis*, Dean of *Lincoln*.
1705   The Rev. Dr. *Stanhope*, Dean of *Canterbury*.
1706 The Rev. Dr. *Kennet*, Archdeacon of *Huntingdon*.
1707 The Reverend Dr. *Gaſtrel*, Canon of *Chriſt-Church, Oxford*.
1708 The Reverend Dr. *Moſs*.
1709 The Reverend Dr. *Bradford*.
1710 The Reverend Dr. *Smalridge*.
1711 The Reverend Dr. *Snape*.
1712 The Reverend and Right Honourable *George* Lord *Willoughby de Broke*.
1713 The Lord Biſhop of *Cheſter*, Sir *William Dawes*.
1714 The Lord Biſhop of *London*, Dr. *Robinſon*.
1715 The Lord Biſhop of *Lincoln*, Dr. *Wake*.
1716 The Lord Biſhop of *Lincoln*, Dr. *Gibſon*.
1717 The Lord Biſhop of *Saliſbury*, Dr. *Talbot*.
1718 The Reverend Dr. *Lupton*, Prebendary of *Durham*.
1719 The Reverend Dr. *Sherlock*, Dean of *Chicheſter*.

5   1720

Anno

1720 The Reverend Dr. *Knight*.
1721 The Reverend Dr. *Marſhall*.
1722 The Lord Biſhop of *Briſtol*, Dr. *Boulter*.
1723 The Reverend Dr. *Waterland*, Maſter of *Magdalen* College, *Cambridge*.
1724 The Lord Biſhop of *Sodor* and *Mann*, Dr. *Wilſon*.
1725 The Reverend Dr. *Berriman*.
1726 The Reverend Dr. *Mangey*, Prebendary of *Durham*.
1727 The Reverend Dr. *Watſon*.
1728 The Reverend Dr. *Yalden*, Prebendary of *Chulmeigh, Devon*.
1729 The Reverend Dr. *Rogers*.
1730 The Lord Biſhop of *Cheſter*, Dr. *Peploe*.
1731 The Lord Biſhop of *Gloceſter*, Dr. *Wilcox*.
1732 The Reverend Dr. *Stebbing*.
1733 The Lord Biſhop of *Peterborough*, Dr. *Clavering*.
1734 The Reverend Dr. *Heylyn*.
1735 The Reverend Dr. *Pearce*.
1736 The Reverend Dr. *Denne*, Archdeacon of *Rocheſter*.
1737 The Reverend Dr. *Thomas*.
1738 The Reverend Dr. *Conybeare*, Dean of *Chriſt-Church, Oxon*.
1739 The Lord Biſhop of *St. David*'s, Dr. *Clagett*.
1740 The Reverend Dr. *Thomas*, Dean of *Peterborough*.
1741 The Lord Biſhop of *St. Aſaph*, Dr. *Maddox*.
1742 The Reverend Dr. *Trapp*.
1743 The Lord Biſhop of *Oxford*, Dr. *Secker*.
1744 The Lord Biſhop of *Bangor*, Dr. *Hutton*.
1745 The Lord Biſhop of *Briſtol*, Dr. *Butler*.
1746 The Rev. Dr. *Lavington*, Reſidentiary of St. *Paul*'s.
1747 The Lord Biſhop of *St. David*'s, Dr. *Trevor*.
1748 The Reverend Dr. *Bearcroft*.
1749 The Reverend Mr. *Squire*, Archdeacon of *Bath*.
1750 The Rev. Mr. *Yardley*, Archdeacon of *Cardigan*.
1751 The Rev. Dr. *Church*, Prebendary of St. *Paul*'s.
1752 The Rev. Dr. *Chapman*, Archdeacon of *Sudbury*.
1753 The Lord Biſhop of *St. Aſaph*, Dr. *Drummond*.
1754 The Reverend Dr. *Colden*, Archdeacon of *London*.

1755

0

Anno

1755 The Lord Bifhop of *Norwich*, Dr. *Hayter*.
1756 The Rev. Dr. *Nicolls*, Mafter of the *Temple*.
1757 The Rev. Mr. *Glocefter Ridley*.
1758 The Rev. Dr. *Dodwell*, Canon Refidentiary of *Sarum*.
1759 The Rev. Dr. *Burton*, Fellow of *Eton* College.
1760 The Rev. Dr. *Afhton*, Fellow of *Eton* College.
1761 The Rev. Mr. *Negus*.
1762 The Lord Bifhop of *Litchfield* and *Coventry*, Dr. *Fred. Cornwallis*.
1763 The Rev. Dr. *Delany*, Dean of *Down*.
1764 The Rev. Sir *Peter Rivers*, Bart.
1765 The Lord Bifhop of *Briftol*, Dr. *Newton*.
1766 The Rev. Dr. *Tucker*, Dean of *Glocefter*.
1767 The Lord Bifhop of *Chefter*, Dr. *Keene*.
1768 The Rev. Dr. *Worthington*, Prebendary of *York*.
1769 The Lord Bifhop of *Norwich*, Dr. *Yonge*.
1770 The Rev. Dr. *Richard Eyre*.
1771 The Rev. Dr. *James Hallifax*.
1772 The Rev. Dr. *Bentham*, Regius Profeffor of Divinity, *Oxford*.
1773 The Lord Bifhop of *Lincoln*, Dr. *Green*.
1774 The Rev. Dr. *Finch*.
1775 The Rev. Dr. *Ogle*, Dean of *Winchefter*.
1776 The Rev. Dr *Kaye*, Sub-Almoner to His Majefty.
1777 The Lord Bifhop of St. *Afaph*, Dr. *Shipley*.
1778 The Rev. Dr. *Hamilton*, Archdeacon of *Colchefter*.
1779 The Rev. Dr. *Robert Markham*.
1780 The Lord Bifhop of *Oxford*, Dr. *Butler*.
1781 The Rev. Dr. *Parker*, Rector of St. *James's, Weftminfter*.
1782 The Lord Bifhop of *Chefter*, Dr. *Porteus*.
1783 The Rev. Dr. *Horne*, Dean of *Canterbury*.
1784 The Rev. Dr. *Vincent*, Sub-Almoner to His Majefty.
1785 The Lord Bifhop of *Ely*, Dr. *Yorke*.
1786 The Lord Bifhop of *Peterborough*, Dr. *Hinchcliffe*.
1787 The Rev. Dr. *Chelfum*, Rector of *Droxford, Hants*.
1788 The Lord Bifhop of *Norwich*, Dr. *Bagot*.
1789 The Lord Bifhop of St. *Afaph*, Dr. *Halifax*.

6
1790

Anno

1790 The Lord Bifhop of *Winchefter*, Dr. *North.*
1791 The Rev. Dr. *Glaffe*, Chaplain in Ord. to his Majefty.
1792 The Lord Bifhop of *Bangor*, Dr. *Warren.*
1793 The Lord Bifhop of St. *David's*, Dr. *Horfley.*
1794 The Rev. Mr. *Pott*, Archdeacon of St. *Alban's.*
1795 The Lord Bifhop of *Briftol*, Dr. *Courtenay.*
1796 The Rev. Dr. *Huntingford*, Warden of *Winchefter*
College.
1797 The Rev. Dr. *Law*, Archdeacon of *Rochefter.*
1798 The Rev. Dr. *Whitfeld*, Rector of St. *Margaret,*
Lothbury.
1799 The Rev. Dr. *Rennell*, Mafter of the *Temple.*

F I N I S.

Printed by Ann Rivington, St. John's Square, Clerkenwell.

.

www.ingramcontent.com/pod-product-compliance
Lightning Source LLC
Chambersburg PA
CBHW030841270326
41928CB00007B/1165